Poetry on a Plate

This collection was edited and designed by a panel of Poetry Society staff, including: Jules Mann, Director (who worked in the wine business in California for 15 years); Janet Phillips, Book Designer; Angel Dahouk, who researched and categorised the poems; Andrew Bailey, who assisted in the research and virtual component of this project; and Jessica York and Valeria Melchioretto who compiled the Poetry Café menu and blackboard.

Poetry on a plate

A feast of poems and recipes

Second Edition

Edited by the Poetry Society

SALT

CAMBRIDGE

PUBLISHED BY SALT PUBLISHING
PO Box 937, Great Wilbraham, Cambridge PDO cb1 5jx United Kingdom

Selection and introduction © Jules Mann, 2004, 2006
Copyright of the poems and recipes rests with the authors and other rights holders
as cited in the acknowledgements.

The right of Jules Mann to be identified as the
editor of this work has been asserted by her in accordance
with Section 77 of the Copyright, Designs and Patents Act 1988.

First edition published 2004
Second edition 2006

Printed and bound in the United Kingdom by Lightning Source

Typeset in Berthold Bodoni 10 / 13

ISBN-13 978 1 84471 114 7 paperback
ISBN-10 1 84471 114 5 paperback

SP

1 3 5 7 9 8 6 4 2

CONTENTS

INTRODUCTION

It has been a delight to produce this book, and I'd like to introduce *Poetry on a Plate* with a glimpse of what went on behind the scenes. It was, at times, as chaotic as the best moments when everything happens all at once in a kitchen; it also allowed those long reflective spaces of imagining particular combinations of flavour, savouring a recipe or poem (even if it wasn't eventually included), and generally immersing ourselves in the sensory realms of poetry and food.

Poetry on a Plate came about because of National Poetry Day, an annual celebration (since 1994) of the art form of poetry. Each year the Poetry Society and our partners work with a particular theme. The theme of 'food' allowed us to explore the creative impulse for both poets and chefs. It enabled us to form some new and, I hope, enduring alliances—it certainly sparked some wonderful responses from those chefs and food writers we approached about the relationship between food and poetry.

It also involved corresponding with poets and writers around the country, fishing for their favourite food poems, either their own or a recommendation of other poets' work. Wendy Cope responded quickly by saying she didn't tend to like food poetry but made an unqualified exception for "Extra Helpings" by Douglas Dunn and "Greedyguts" by Kit Wright, with its refrain line, "The bigger the breakfast, the larger the lunch". Paul Farley admitted, "I wouldn't wear a chef's hat or suffer a bollocking from Gordon Ramsay, but ideas of cuisine, high and low, interest me". John Mole mulled, "Where to begin? Food as necessity, indulgence, largesse, eroticism, nostalgia, political analogy, character definition . . . ? And that would probably be a mere aperitif". Philip Gross proposed that "whether or not one goes along with the Christian metaphors, that way of linking the most good and basic things (bread) with the highest/deepest (spirituality, poetry) seems right to me". Deryn Rees-Jones pointed out the fact that Grevel Lindop's poem 'Summer Pudding' does actually work as a recipe, and noted the tradition of great cooks who were also poets—Elizabeth Bishop among them. On the other end of the spectrum, 'Mushrooms' by Sylvia Plath was recommended by Professor Ann Oakley, who says the poem "doesn't make you want to eat them, but on the other hand some food is really quite creepy!".

William Sieghart, founder of National Poetry Day, read me some wonderful examples of his favourite ("intriguing") food poems, some of which are included here; of those that are not, it's worth hunting down John Burnside's 'The Asylum Dance' and Gillian Clarke's 'Anorexic'. In fact, if you'd like to view an entire bookshelf of food poems, have a browse on the Poetry Society's website (www.poetrysociety.org.uk/food).

I would like to thank the chefs, poets, and their publishers who, by contributing their recipes and poems, will help sustain future National Poetry Days. Thanks also to our partners in poetry who contributed to the National Poetry Day menu in the last section. The first edition of this book was made possible by the generous support of Salt Publishing and funding from Arts Council England. The Second Edition incorporates some wonderful recipes and poems that arrived too late for the first printing, but were so good we decided to publish an updated edition. A typical example is the Joachim Ringelnatz poem 'Ich habe Dich so lieb' that Antonio Carluccio sent us, which reminded him of living in Germany between 1962 and 1975; all he could remember was the first part, 'Ich habe Dich so lieb / Ich würde Dir ohne Bedenken / Eine Kachel aus meinem Ofen / schenken' which is translated by Ernest A. Seemann as 'I love you so! / I would, without any regret / Give you a mattress spring / Of my bed.' which rather puzzled us until we tracked down the rest of the poem which ends: 'Ich lache. / Die Löcher sind die Hauptsache / An einem Sieb. / Ich habe Dich so lieb.' In translation: 'I laugh. / Caviar is an epitaph / On sturgeon's roe. / I love you so.'

Finally, this book owes everything to the enthusiasm of my colleagues at the Poetry Society, in particular Janet Phillips for keep-

ing us on course, Andrew Bailey and Ripa Haque for eagle-eyed edit-
ing, and Angel Dahouk who is now a walking encyclopaedia of food
poems.

Enjoy your poetry on a plate.

JULES MANN

A Visit to the Poetry Café

JESSICA YORK

Poetry Café Manager and Cook

WELCOME TO THE POETRY CAFÉ, LONDON

Food and poetry come together quite simply at the Poetry Café.

From behind the counter we can watch customers running through the blackboard with this week's poem on it before realising that they meant to read the menu in the second blackboard above the bar. Hard to tell sometimes which tempts them the most . . .

The *TLS* (*Times Literary Supplement*) used to needle us for having no poetry in sight – "call yourself a poetry café?" – but now there is a board with all the recent press clippings about poetry, other boards advertising our own and everyone else's events, as well as a rotating selection of young artists' work on the walls and a clientele prone to think deep thoughts over blank sheets of paper.

We have been permutating poetry and food for the last six years, without making too exaggerated a claim for the lyricism of our own cooking. One of the most memorable ways of putting the two together has been to ask poets who love cooking (and lots of them do), to cook a great meal for a long table full of customers and to host the evening.

Many great poets/cooks have now done so. I have to say, some well-known poets have also declined the invitation for the greater good of our customers. So cookery doesn't always go hand-in-hand with writing, though I suspect good eating often does.

MATTHEW SWEENEY
"Dinner with . . ." Poet in the Café

SALATĂ DE VINETE, OR AUBERGINE SALAD

A delicious but simple summer starter in Romania — summer because
vegetables are still seasonal there, and all the better for that. The best
I had was in a good restaurant on the Black Sea, where one could
taste that the aubergines had been roasted on the grill.

Ingredients:
3 — 4 large aubergines
1 medium sized onion
Sunflower oil
Salt

SERVES 2 OR MORE

Cook the aubergines on the hot grill, turning all the time. (If you do
not have a grill you can bake them in the oven, or on a hot plate put
directly onto the stove or gas flame, but the result will not be as
good.) When they are blackened all over and beginning to go soft,
peel and drain them. Then chop them on a wooden board, using a
wooden or plastic cleaver if possible, and put into a bowl. Peel and
chop the onion very finely, and add to the bowl, along with salt to
taste. Mix thoroughly. Add oil, a little bit at a time, until the mixture
attains the consistency of mayonnaise.

Some people actually add mayonnaise, but this is not traditional,
and the dish doesn't need it. The customary way to serve it is with
sliced tomatoes, or an attractive variant is to slice large tomatoes in
half horizontally, squeeze the juice and seeds out, and stuff the halves
with the aubergine mixture.

MATTHEW SWEENEY

EGG

Ask in a beach café for a boiled egg
and it comes raw — well, it's hot
but when your hands grow oven gloves
to prise the shell off in shards
a fissure forms and liquid white
drops out, leaving a clear glimpse
of raw yolk. You call the waiter,
tell him it's *not boiled* — you can't
eat this with a knife & fork! He agrees,
instigates a replacement. It comes,
eventually, and is even hotter,
a real test of the asbestos fingers,
but the shell comes off, with the egg
intact, until the knife attacks it,
meeting — you can't believe it — *soft yolk*
which floods out onto your plate,
with not an egg-spoon in sight.
You do your best to eat it, but run —
a safe hour later — into the sea
and swallow as much of the salty water
as you can — the extra salty water,
one should say, this being the Black Sea.
Egg-taste recurs all day. That evening
you order, in a restaurant, pork stew
with polenta — a safe choice, you think,
till it arrives with a local variant
your lack of the language blocks you from:
a soft fried egg sitting there on top!

SARAH MAGUIRE
"Dinner with . . ." Poet in the Café

THYME SALAD
Salatet al-zaatar al-akhdar

Thyme grows in abundance all over the Levant, and it is the plant most powerfully associated with Palestine. It's commonly eaten for breakfast: warm flat bread is dipped into olive oil and then into a bowl of *zaatar* — a rough, pungent mixture of crushed, dried thyme leaves combined with sumac (the dried berry of the *sumac* tree, ground into a dark red powder with a sour, lemony flavour), toasted sesame seeds and salt. Packets of *zaatar* can be found in Middle Eastern grocery stores; I rather like it on toast.

This salad, however, is made with fresh thyme leaves. These little woody bundles again can be found in Middle Eastern stores, and in Greek and West Indian grocers too; the new season begins in late April but you can usually buy fresh thyme throughout the year. I made Thyme Salad as one of the *mezze* for my dinner at the Poetry Café; everyone was intrigued by its sharp, pungent flavour. It's too powerful to be eaten alone, and is best served with a number of other *mezze*, good bread, and some sharp green olives.

SERVES 4 AS APPETISER

IN A BOWL, crush 1 clove of garlic with salt into a puree; stir in the juice of 1 lemon and 2–3 tablespoons of extra virgin olive oil; whisk these together vigorously. Then add the leaves stripped from 1 bunch of fresh thyme and 1 medium onion, finely chopped. Simple and wonderful.

SARAH MAGUIRE

Zaatar

for Zakaria Mohammed

Astringent, aromatic, antiseptic –
the souls of the dead
come to rest in the blooms
of this bitter herb

to haunt the bleached landscape
of limestone
of broken stones
of olive trees stricken and wasted

Incendiary – a volatile oil
can be crushed from its leaves
small pockets of scent
toughened, hirsute

Uprooted, exploded
ground under foot
its pungency rises
staining the air –

pollen like gunpowder
dust in the hand
cast over Palestine
from the mouths of stones

MIMI KHALVATI
"Dinner with . . ." Poet in the Café

KORESHT BADEMJAN

Ingredients:
1 free range chicken
1 large onion
3 cloves garlic
1 teaspoon turmeric
2 teaspoon cinnamon
1 lb dried walnuts
1 large cup of pomegranate purée (available from Iranian groceries)
Cooking oil

SERVES 2

BOIL THE CHICKEN with a little salt to make stock. Cut and bone the cooled chicken if you like. Chop the onions and garlic. Fry slowly in oil (in a saucepan or casserole dish, not a frying pan) so as to caramelise the onion, then add turmeric. Add the chicken portions and pour in chicken stock. Put on low heat to simmer. Grind the walnuts finely and add them, little by little, to the pot. Keep stirring When all the walnuts are well mixed in, put the lid on and simmer for half an hour. Add the cinnamon and pomegranate purée, stir and simmer for another 10 minutes. Serve with steamed Basmati rice. This dish can also be made with pheasant or duck.

Mimi Khalvati was one of the Poetry Café's first poets to be asked to cook in the "Dinner with . . ." series; she brought her secret ingredient, which was her mother, to cook up a Persian feast. This is her mother's recipe.

MIMI KHALVATI

HAIKU

On the verandah
the wet-nurse thinks of her own
pomegranate tree.

JOHN HEGLEY

"Dinner with . . ." Poet in the Café

THE CUSTOMER'S COMPLAINT

In the caff
swapping some of her spaghetti
for a bit of his moussaka
she considered what a benefit it was having a
         partner
when you both wanted the same two
separate meals on the menu.
Unfortunately she considered it
to be the only benefit.

NII AYIKWEI PARKES
"Dinner with . . ." Poet in the Café

DEEP FRIED YAM WITH AVOCADO KPAKPO SHITO

This is a recipe I developed as a modification to a popular Ghanaian snack of fried yam and kpakpo shito (crushed pepper dip). The avocado cuts the spiciness of the pepper and gives the dip a cool twist.

Ingredients:
1 tuber of sweet yam (ask for 'Puna' yam at an African market)
4 medium-sized fresh tomatoes
½ teaspoon of salt (maximum – should ideally be done to taste)
1 small soft avocado
½ a lime
1 large onion
3–7 kpakpo shito (Small Scotch Bonnet peppers – you may use the bigger ones but adjust the amount of pepper according to taste)
Oil for frying

SERVES 2–3

PEEL THE YAM and slice it into bite-sized chips (thick cut). Sprinkle the yam with a little bit of salt and deep fry until tender in the middle. Ideally, wait until the oil is hot (about 180°C) before putting the yam in to fry otherwise you will get soggy chips.

While the yam chips are frying, peel and cut the onion into four quarters and place the tomatoes, kpakpo shito, ½ of the onion and some salt into a blender and liquidise. When the mix is smooth, peel and add the avocado and squeeze in the lime (this is to prevent the avocado oxidising, but it plays a dual role and adds a zing to the dip). Finally, chop the remaining quarter of the onion finely to garnish the dip.

Serve the dip in a small bowl placed in centre of a plate of chips. Serves 2–3 Ghanaians.

Note from the poet: the only food poems I have published are 'The Bite' in my first collection *Eyes of a Boy, Lips of a Man*, and 'Orange Flesh' in *Wasafiri*.

JOHN AGARD
"Dinner with . . ." Poet in the Café

BEHIND THE MENU

Sweet and Sour
moved in next door
to Fish and Chips.

And farther down the street,
Naan Bread and Curry
were neighbours to Rice and Peas.

But with time, these families
got into a hullabaloo —
or should that be a vindaloo —

when the only boy
of Naan Bread and Curry chose
the Fish and Chips girl to marry.

And the Sweet and Sour youngest
ran off one summer
with the Rice and Peas eldest.

Is there a happy
ending to this story?
That would be telling.

Let's just say they got together
to sort out their grumbles
over apple crumble

and to discuss the loud couple
just moved into number three —
Bolognese and Spaghetti.

VALERIA MELCHIORETTO
Poet, artist and waitstaff at the Poetry Café

BRIDGING GAPS BETWEEN BLACKBOARDS

It you have ever visited the Poetry Café you will know that we have two constantly changing blackboards — the menu and the poem board. The first is to engage the imagination for the lovely food options on offer and tease the taste buds, while the other, smaller board holds a few lines of poetry to activate the appetite for one or many tasty poems from the magazines or books on the shelves or freshly-read by the poets themselves in our basement.

We take care and time over the writing of both these boards. It is quite tricky to capture the complex experience that a meal might hold. For example, should the Strawberry Tomato Soup be best described as spicy, sweet or semi-sensational? You've just got to try it.

The poem board, on the other hand, is spice for the mind, words to melt on the tongue. By picking a few lines from a complete poem, there is a danger of over-emphasising a subjective nuance which can alter the original meaning. It is as delicate as making a soufflé for which a few eggs must be broken. However, it is striking that you can dip into almost any poetry book and scoop rich food references, metaphors and similes. Poetry and food are as close as the princess and the pea, as urgent as cause and effect. Here are a few samples of popular dishes at the Poetry Café in relation to 'blackboard poems' to accentuate their flavour.

CHILLED BEETROOT AND APPLE SOUP

. . .
Eve ate Adam.
The serpent ate Eve,
This is the dark intestine.

. . . from 'Theology' by Ted Hughes. This dish is the ultimate temptation that starts off any exciting meal: sweet, cool and vibrant.

Egyptian Spinach and Lentil Soup

I always bragged
about your soup
I think that's what
attracted me
to you, that hot soup.

... from 'Soup of Venus' by James Tate. A soup made with so much love, one would think Venus, the goddess of love herself, had put the apron on.

Caramelised Onion Soup

Generous,
you dissolve
your globe of freshness
is fervently
consumed in the stew pot
and the crystal shred
kindled by the heat of the oil
turns into a curly golden feather.

... from 'Ode to the Onion' by Pablo Neruda (see also page 32). This soup is deliciously rich in flavour as well as being light and fresh. It prepares you for take-off.

Frittata and Salad

Now when the center bubbles thickly
spoon in the mushroom and onion mixture —

though the Platonic ideal omelette
has only hot, loose egg at its heart, with fresh
herbs, like the one Lamber Strether
lunched on, and fell for that lost French lady.

. . . from 'Omelette' by Marilyn Hacker. A main course which tastes
even better if you eat it in the company of someone special.

Quiche served with New Potatoes

He smiles
And slowly he eats
The book of the lord of the world

. . . from 'St. Sava's School' by Vasko Popa. A dish you can't go wrong
with, always satisfying, filling and restoring all round.

BAKED HALLOUMI WITH PUY LENTILS AND TOMATO SAUCE

then it is time, after much stirring
and some contemplation

to find the appropriate tune
perhaps one of Schubert's final sonatas

. . . from 'Diablo: A Recipe' by August Kleinzahler. This dish mobilises the senses and has almost musical qualities.

SUMMER FRUIT CRUMBLE

I love to go out in late September
among the fat, overripe, icy, black blackberries
to eat blackberries for breakfast

. . . from 'Blackberry Eating' by Galway Kinnell. Not just for breakfast but for lunch and dinner too. The Summer Fruit Crumble is a piece of art.

APRICOT TART

. . . Don't rub
the stain from the cloth. It's good to know:
people were here before me.

. . . from 'Instructions for a Waitress' by Yehuda Amichai. A special treat. There are usually no traces of crumbs left behind . . . only a perfectly empty plate.

SUE RITCHIE
Poetry Café Cook

CHILLED BEETROOT AND APPLE SOUP

Ingredients:
1 lb (500 g) cooked, peeled beetroot
Juice of one lemon
1½ pints (850 ml) unsweetened apple juice, chilled
10 oz (300 g) Greek-style yoghurt or crème fraîche
Salt and pepper
4 inch (10 cm) piece cucumber
6 fresh mint leaves
6–8 fresh chives
Cayenne pepper, to taste

To serve:
Chives and mint sprigs to garnish

SERVES 4

SLICE THE BEETROOT and place in a food processor or blender. Add the lemon juice, half the apple juice and half the yoghurt. Process for 1–2 minutes until smooth.

Pour the beetroot mixture into a mixing bowl, stir in the rest of the apple juice and season with cayenne, salt and pepper to taste. Chill until ready to serve, then pour into individual soup bowls.

To make the cucumber cream, grate the cucumber and stir into the remaining yoghurt. Chop the mint and stir into the mixture. Spoon some cucumber cream into the middle of each serving and sprinkle with a little cayenne pepper. Snip some chives over the top and garnish with mint.

JESSICA YORK
Poetry Café Manager and Cook

EGYPTIAN SPINACH AND LENTIL SOUP

Ingredients:
8 oz (250 g) red lentils
1 bunch of spinach
1 teaspoon of cumin seed
1 medium Spanish onion
Olive oil
Seasoning
2 litres stock

SERVES 5

CHOP THE ONION and fry gently in the olive oil. Add the cumin seeds and fry them with the onion.

When the onion is soft and translucent, add the lentils, seasoning and stock. Bring to the boil and simmer for 20 minutes or until the lentils are thoroughly soft.

Meanwhile, wash the spinach thoroughly, chop roughly and add to the soup.

Adjust seasoning—add more cumin if flavour has become too subtle. (If you do, cook for a little longer to allow the flavour to integrate!)

You can also adjust the thickness by adding more (or less) liquid to get your preferred consistency.

RACHEL ROBB
Poetry Café Cook

SPICY CARAMELIZED RED ONION SOUP

Ingredients:
6 good sized red onions
2½ pints (1½ litres) vegetable stock, (either fresh, or 2 heaped teaspoons of Swiss Marigold bouillon in water)
½ teaspoon Turkish red pepper flakes (or more to taste) or a good pinch of cayenne
Juice of ½ a lemon
2 tablespoon of olive oil
Knob of butter (optional)
Handful of parsley
Salt and pepper

SERVES 6

SLICE ONIONS THINLY and fry them in oil (and butter) on a low heat for approximately 40 minutes, allowing to brown.
   Add vegetable stock and bring to the boil.
   Add lemon juice, red pepper flakes and parsley.
   Simmer for an extra 10 minutes.
   Season to taste.

RACHEL ROBB
Poetry Café Cook

BAKED HALLOUMI WITH PUY LENTILS AND TOMATO SAUCE

Ingredients:
8 oz (250 g) of puy lentils (rinsed)
1 onion
1 clove of garlic
2 tablespoon of balsamic vinegar
4 tablespoon of olive oil
Juice of one lemon
2 × 8 oz (250 g) packs of halloumi

For the sauce:
2 cloves of garlic
1 onion
2 × 14 oz (400 g) cans of tomatoes
Handful of fresh thyme or basil, or both

SERVES 6 (APPROX)

For the lentils, fry one onion – add rinsed lentils and cook at a low temperature in ¾ pint (400 ml) of water (you may need to add more towards the end) for 45 minutes or until tender.

For the sauce, fry thin slivers of garlic and onion and cook gently for 30–40 minutes, reducing to a thick sauce. Add the rest of the herbs.

Cut the halloumi lengthways in 1½ cm slices, bake in the oven with generous amounts of oil for 20 minutes at medium heat. When the lentils are ready, drain off any excess oil, put back in the pan (turning off the heat), and add crushed garlic, lemon juice, balsamic vinegar and olive oil.

Season to taste.

For serving, spoon out the lentils, top with sauce and lay halloumi slabs over the top.

JESSICA YORK
Poetry Café Manager and Cook

APRICOT AND ALMOND CRUMBLE

I have a feeling this originated from Jane Grigson but, like all good recipes, it now feels thoroughly my own. I like crumbles that have lots of fruit, are not very sweet and only have a thin layer of crumble.

Ingredients:
1½ lb (750 g) fresh apricots
8 oz (250 g) plain flour
3½ oz (100 g) ground almonds
3½ oz (100 g) flaked almonds
4 oz (125 g) butter
3½ oz (100 g) sugar
crème fraîche (optional)

SERVES 4–6

Stone the apricots and put them in an 12 x 8 inch (20 x 30 cm) oblong oven-proof dish or something similar. Sprinkle half the sugar on them. Light the oven on gas mark 5 (375° F, 190° C) and let it warm up.

Put the flour, ground almonds, butter, and half the sugar in a bowl and rub the fat into the dry ingredients as you would to make pastry. When the crumble is the consistency of fine bread crumbs, sprinkle it evenly over the top of the apricots to seal in the juices.

Cover the crumble with flaked almonds and put in the oven. Cook for 25 minutes or until the top is browning

Serve with crème fraîche. It's a great combination.

Poetry on a Plate —
a feast of recipes and poems

SIMON SMITH, TRANSLATOR

Horace: On Drinking your Good Health

You'll be sipping wine in regular measure,
A modest little Sabine which I fixed myself
In Greek amphorae shelved that very day applause
    Echoed round the theatre

For you, round the Vatican hill Maecenas,
The illustrious one, to your forebears' riverside,
Repeating back a welcome return, resounding
    In news of your good health.

Drink the Caecuban and Calenian fine wines
As you wish round your place, but my glasses know not
The refinements of the Formian mountainsides
    Nor Falernian groves.

Notes from the translator:
Poem: Horace, *Odes* Book I.20.
Maecenas is a friend of Emperor Augustus, and patron of poets (Horace being one
of them).

MICHAEL MURPHY

OVID IN AN ENGLISH KITCHEN-GARDEN

> *While the limbs were still warm, and still retained*
> *some vestiges of life, they cooked the flesh, boiling*
> *some in pots, roasting some on spits.*
> METAMORPHOSES, BOOK VI

Water seethes. It has murder on the brain.
Tubers ripped from beds, heads shaved clean
with a switch from a kitchen knife
and no more malice than you'd bring to bear
on the choice of wine. In my exactitude
I'm watching as, bruising herbs with a deft
flick of the wrist, you remember
tonight's guests are squeamish about fish
and must top-and-tail the sea-farmed trout
before melting in a skillet an ounce of butter,
sauté-ing carrots and celery until just so.
Truite au Bleu. Chunks of flesh-on-the-bone
disguised in a court bouillon
and, with a shot of vermouth, served cold.

Note from the author: this poem springs from the idea that Ovid's *Metamorphoses*
has some claim to being called the first cookery book!

JOHN MOLE

THE BANQUET

'Grub first then ethics' said Brecht
When the going was tough
As for many it always is
And fine words are never enough.

Presuming at least to offer
Food for the mind,
He wrote about hunger
Of a different kind.

What, despite the consoling
Banquet of art,
Can an empty belly
Say to a broken heart?

Poetry makes nothing happen
As Auden insisted;
Its flow is not water,
It can't bake bread

Yet it measures out hope
In a global cup
And against all the odds
Will not give up.

Appetisers

FRANCES WILLIAMS

Oyster Eating

Luxury doesn't get more
Astringent. Plucked from
Cloudy depths, my plate
Of oysters wait for their
Moment, little glaciers
In silky cups. I suck

An avalanche of flesh.
Then clear my throat
Of their strange salt
Swallow, more touch
Than taste. Out of these
Rocky skulls, the brains

Come slippery as sex.
Each one tips over the
Rugged callused lips of
Its single shoe to speak
Only with the one tongue,
A probe both first and

Last. Such rash
Adventurers. Jonahs
In my whale. And also
Something sad in our
Hurried consummation.
A dozen down, I reach

A check-mate moment
In this game of numbers.
As Casanova, on a lucky
Night, might break a line
Of kisses, to pause for breath
On heaven's racing staircase.

SARAH WARDLE

WORD TASTING

First agitate the word in your glass,
swilling it around anti-clockwise
to let the air into the language.

Tilt the glass against the tablecloth.
Notice the colour. Is this word golden
or brick-red? Does the nose remind you

of freshly-mown grass or tropical fruit?
Is the word smoky or woody on the palate?
Do the syllables have a long aftertaste?

Has the word been aged? Do you like it?
Now try this. It is a controversial word,
the oldest vintage known to man. The seeds

can be used to grow this word in Europe
or the New World. Each climate gives
the word a different flavour. It's versatile,

easily turned into language. Growers love it
across the financial spectrum. Many find
this word smooth and buttery, fruity and ripe.

They say it is an alpha word, their favourite.
Some drink it early and often, others will
store it in their cellars for drinking later.

Then again, still others find the word bitter
and acidic, screwing up their faces, saying
it reminds them of cat's pee on gooseberry bushes.

There's no accounting for taste. Make up
your own mind. What does it remind you of?
In the beginning the label said *God*.

Tempura of Aubergine and Courgette with Caviar

The flavour of the tempura and the fresh, deep-fried vegetables goes perfectly with caviar.

Ingredients
1 slim aubergine
Salt
1 medium courgette
Light oil for deep-frying (sunflower or vegetable)
½ Red onion, finely chopped
3½ oz (100g) Oscietre or Beluga caviar
3½ fl oz (100ml) Crème fraîche

Batter
5 fl oz (150ml) Cold water
3½ oz (100g) Plain flour
Salt and freshly ground black pepper

Serves 4

1. CUT THE AUBERGINE into thin slices. Sprinkle salt on both sides and leave for 30 minutes. Rinse well, then drain on kitchen paper. Peel and slice the courgette.

2. To make the batter, mix together the water, flour and a pinch of salt and pepper in a pudding bowl. The batter should be thick enough to stick to the vegetable slices, but not too thick.

3. Heat 2 fl oz (50ml) of oil in a frying pan. Dip the slices of aubergine and courgette into the batter and fry immediately, until lightly golden on both sides (it is easy to burn these, so watch them carefully). Remove with a slotted spoon, drain well on kitchen paper and keep warm. You may need to do two or three batches, depending on the size of your frying pan.

4. Taking four warm plates, arrange an equal number of fried aubergine and courgette slices around the edges. Sprinkle with a little chopped onion and top each with crème fraîche and a small teaspoon of caviar.

Serve with Sancerre/Pouilly-Fume, New Zealand Sauvignon or Clare Valley Riesling.

OWEN SHEERS

HEDGE SCHOOL

> *"Though that hir soules goon a-blakeberyed"*
> CHAUCER, *The Pardoner's Prologue*

The walk home from school got longer
during those first weeks of September,
listening to the mini bus diminish
through the hedges, muffled by trees,
then slipping the straps of my bag over each shoulder
to free up both hands for the picking of blackberries.

Another lesson perhaps, this choice of how to take them.
One by one, tracing their variety on my tongue,
from the bitterness of an unripe red,
tightly packed as a nervous heart,
to the rain-bloated looseness of those older,
cobwebbed and dusty as a Claret
laid down for years in a cellar.

Or to hoard them? Piling in the palm
until I cupped a coiled black pearl necklace,
a hedgerow caviar, the bubbles of just poured wine
stilled in my fingers which I'd take together,
each an eye of one great berry, a sudden symphony.

Or, as I did just once, strolling towards the low house
growing at the lane's end,
not to eat them at all,
but slowly close my palm into a fist instead,
dissolving their mouthfeel over my skin
and emerging from the hedge and tree tunnel
my knuckles scratched and my hand blue−black red,

as bloodied as a butcher's or a farmer's at lambing
or that of a boy who has discovered for the very first time
just how dark he runs inside.

This was written in response to the cards Heston Blumenthal puts on his tables
asking diners to tell him about 'Nostalgia Foods' – the tastes and sensations that
remind them of places, their youth etc. For Heston these seem to often be artifi-
cial flavours – Sherbet Dips, Pink Panther chocolate bars, but for me it really had
to be blackberries. Heston is very interested in our early taste experiences so I
also wanted to write something that drew from childhood/adolescence.

He also has interesting ideas about 'Flavour Memory' which seemed to me a
perfect phrase for what a poet tries to achieve in a poem – so I suppose I hope
this in an example of such a flavour memory.

I was very struck by how Heston spoke about food, and to this end I wanted to
include some of his phrases – such as 'mouthfeel' – the sensation/texture a food
has on our tongues – and even the use of the word 'Symphony', which is one
Heston often uses to describe the complete tasting experience.

The quotation from 'The Pardoner's Prologue' is, I think, well known and carries
its own connotations . . .

ANTON EDELMANN

Allium Restaurant, London, England

SHALLOT TART WITH GOAT'S CHEESE

Ingredients:
2 crottin de chavignol (or a similar form of goat's cheese)
⅓ pint (200 ml) olive oil
3 garlic cloves
1 sprig of thyme
1 sprig of rosemary
7 oz (200 g) puff pastry
35 oz (1 kg) shallots, peeled
⅔ pint (400 ml) chicken stock
Basil oil (see recipe)
2 fl oz (50 ml) balsamic vinegar
Salt and black pepper mill

CUT THE CHEESE in half and place in the olive oil with the garlic, rosemary and thyme. Marinate for at least four hours or overnight for extra flavour. Remove and dry.

Heat a little of the oil from the cheese in a double-bottomed pan and place the shallots inside. The shallots should just cover the bottom of the pan – there should not be any free space, neither should they be on top of each other. Fry until coloured on all sides and pour away the oil, then add the chicken stock. Simmer on the stove until the jus has reduced, then cover and place in the oven. Braise until they are cooked well at gas mark 3 (325° F, 160° C) approximately 45 minutes. Remove and divide the shallots into 4 inch (10 cm) wide non-stick moulds.

Roll out the puff pastry until approximately ½ mm thick and cut out 10 cm discs.

Place on top of the shallots and bake in the oven at 200° C (400° F), until the puff pastry is golden brown (approximately 20 minutes).

Turn out on a plate.

Allium: (Large genus of perennial and biennial pungent bulbous plants with strongly scented cylindrical basal leaves and star shaper flowers in an umble on a leafless stem: garlic; leek; onion; chive.)

Grill the goat's cheese until slightly brown and hot. Place on top of the tart. Drizzle a little basil oil and the balsamic vinegar around the dish.

To make the Basil Oil:
1¾ pints (1 litre) olive oil
35 oz (1 kg) basil

Pick basil leaves from stalks, blanch and refresh in iced water. Squeeze dry and place all ingredients in robot-coupe — blitz for 25 minutes. Push through chinois, making sure you get every drop out. Allow to drain through two coffee filters, and store in kilner jars.

ANTON EDELMANN, chef of Allium Restaurant, is particularly fond of the following selection of poems on the theme of 'Onions'. . .

LEEKES

If Leekes you like, but do their smell dis-like,
Eat Onyons, and you shall not smell the Leeke;
If you of Onyons would the scent expell,
Eat Garlicke, that shall drowne the Onyons' smell.

from 'The Cook's Oracle', by DR WILLIAM KITCHINER

ONYONS

This is every cook's opinion —
No savory dish without an onion,
But lest your kissing should be spoiled
Your onions must be fully boiled.

from The Poems of JONATHAN SWIFT

In addition to these, he also mentions:

'Onions', by Lorna Crozier, which begins:

The onion loves the onion.
It hugs its many layers,
. . .

and 'Ode to an Onion' by Pablo Neruda, which begins:

Onion,
luminous phial,
petal by petal
your beauty was formed,

. . . and ends as follows:

a celestial globe, cup of platinum,
motionless dance
of anemone covered in snow
and the fragrance of earth
lives in your crystalline nature.

(See also page 13.)

NEIL ROLLINSON

ONIONS

"Mine eyes smell onions, I shall weep anon."

It's enough to bring tears to your eyes
this talk of a modified onion, tamed
and impotent, shorn of its magic properties,
the power to make you weep over chutney,
to blub like a baby while making salsa.
You've sharpened your knives and chopped
in goggles, you've vinegared your board,
you've soaked the bulbs, but nothing has helped.

Sacred symbol of the universe,
cure for baldness, dog bites and warts,
steroid for Roman Olympians,
enemy to aphid and carrot fly,
polish for copper and glass.

White Spear, Tokyo Long, Beltsville Bunching,
Walla Walla, Rosa Lunga Di Firenza,
Red Globe, Ebenezer: drying in sheds all winter.

They have graced the chopping boards
of ancient Egypt, Greece, and Mesopotamia,
whose cooks have sobbed in their sculleries,
cursing the spirits who live in the kitchen ceiling
They wept on the Mayflower taking them overseas,
and the Queen of Hearts demanded the head
of the one who brought turnips instead.

So slice it with reverence, cut the green flesh
and watch it bleed. Feel the burn as you take it apart,
this papery ordnance full of tear-gas and milky sap.
Lay down your knife and grip the table,
rock on your heels, like a god
full of human suffering, dream of your supper,
and weep.

SIMON AQUILINA

Writer and Sous Chef, Ynyshir Hall Hotel, Powys, Wales

ARANCINI WITH RED PEPPERS

A delicious and different way to serve risotto. You can serve Arancini as small canapés, as a starter for a dinner party, or accompanied with salad for a light lunch. You can really experiment with the fillings — try using marinated meats, spices and diced vegetables.

For the Arancini:
8 oz (250 g) cooked Arborio risotto rice
3 ½ oz (100 g) poached fish: fresh tuna or salmon, flaked into small pieces
3 tablespoons of chopped coriander
3 tablespoons of finely chopped black olive
1 ½ oz (40 g) buffalo mozzarella, finely diced
1 ½ oz (40 g) finely grated parmesan cheese / seasoning and lemon juice to taste
1 whole egg beaten together — (to bind)

For the pane:
2 oz (50 g) seasoned plain flour
3 whole eggs, beaten together
3 ½ oz (100 g) fine breadcrumbs

For the garnish:
Picked, washed leaves: frisee, wild rocket, tarragon, and coriander
1 red pepper finely diced / olive oil and garlic for cooking
1 tablespoon sherry vinegar

For the dressing:
2 fl oz (60 ml) groundnut oil
1 ¾ fl oz (50ml) arachide oil
¾ fl oz (22ml) white wine vinegar
1 teaspoon sherry vinegar
4 pitted black olives finely diced
2 tablespoons chopped coriander / seasoning and lemon juice to taste

Arancini is a very traditional Maltese specialty,
The fillings — depend on the producer's locality.
In Mosta, they're filled with tomato and cheese,
In Valletta, tuna — even spicy peas.

In Sliema, they come plain with freshly grated Parmesan,
At Luqa, the airport, commercially packed with chopped ham!
In Rabat they are exceptionally big,
In Msida, I've had them sweet, garnished with Maltese fig

In Hamrun, people like them spicy and hot,
Accompanied with sauce, eaten straight from the pot.
Traditional recipes in Buggiba and Qawra,
Include pickled vegetables, which are slightly sour.

Shops in the south, use fresh seafood, like in Marsaskala,
Sold in the high streets, to hungry shoppers — a typical scenario in Birkirkara.
Pumpkin and capers are included at Paradise bay,
Recipes date back, many years, so the locals say!

Enjoyed whilst relaxing in the tranquility of Mdina,
Private cooks, serve them, to wealthy homeowners, in Madliena.
In Poala, the ones served at religious festivals are full of zest,
But, arancini my "Papa" makes — are without doubt the best!

SERVES 2

IN A MEDIUM sized round bottomed bowl, place the cooked risotto rice, add the poached fish, chopped coriander, chopped black olive, diced mozzarella, parmesan and seasoning, mix together thoroughly. Incorporate the egg, using enough just to bind the ingredients together.

Portion the rice into 45g balls and then continue to mould between the palms of your hands, creating a round ball. Place on a tray and refrigerate for one hour.

Prepare the pane, using three small round – bottomed bowls. Pass the molded rice balls through the seasoned flour, then the egg and finally the breadcrumbs. Re-mould the arancini, once they have been bread crumbed – place on a tray until required.

Peel and dice the red pepper, then sauté in olive oil, flavoured with a little garlic. Deglaze with sherry vinegar, lightly season and cook until the pepper is soft.

For the dressing: In a round-bottomed bowl, combine the oils and vinegars and whisk together until emulsified. Add the diced olives, seasoning, and chopped coriander. Wash the lettuce thoroughly, ensuring all dirt and foreign bodies are removed.

To serve, deep-fry the arancini at $325°$ F / $160°$ C for several minutes, until golden brown. Remove and drain the excess oil on paper tissue, remembering to season lightly. On the plate, make five small piles of diced peppers, with a small bouquet of salad and herbs in the middle. Stir the dressing, and then spoon over the salad and around. Place the warm arancini on top of the peppers and serve immediately.

SELIMA HILL

LETTUCES

This poem is a poem about you.
I'm going to lay you down on the bed
and all you have to do is just listen.

I sit beside you on the little chair.
And this in fact is where the poem ends –
just as I'm about to forgive you.

(This poem's getting shorter and shorter.
It used to be a poem about lettuces.
It used to be bright green and irrepressible.)

LEMN SISSAY

Sandwich Love

Triangular sandwiches lounge on plates
They don't guffaw, gawp or gesticulate
They kiss each other lip to salivating lip
They don't posture pose and stylishly sip
They don't have calling cards and though well-dressed
Have no need or will for public address
They just pout at each other, smile and wink
They go down well with drink

Triangular sandwiches all love-struck
Have you ever seen a more glazed blushing cook?
"Slap me with the salmon and pull down the shutters"
"Smother me in butter," another one mutters
"Stroke me down with cucumber slices . . ."
"I like it like that, pepper me with spices,"
"Massage that cream cheese over my chest"
"Let your olive oil seep through my bread vest"

Triangular sandwiches soaked in salad dressing
The lusciously laid lovers among the depressing
Pretenders pretending they're enjoying the chat
Of the who's who in the what's what of where it must be at
The lush lounge lizards lay and like when lovers undo
Stretch by the rosed radish as corks seductively unscrew
But a suit will saunter his hand, will swoop limply from above
He will open his salivating mouth push one in and shove
He will crunch her inside his grating teeth
And leave the other sandwich sandwiched in grief

JOHN JAMES

AFTER FRANCIS AMUNATÉGUI

The appearance
of a hot sausage
with its salad
of potatoes in oil
can leave nobody
indifferent . . .

it is pure, it
precludes
all sentimentality,
it is
the Truth

Mains & Sides

DAVID HARSENT

THE HARE AS LOVE CHARM

Jugged-up she is all dark meat,
weeping from brow to heel. Her eyes are white,

as you can see; a web of veins in the pelt
still runs blue-black. Discard all that. Now draw aside

the blood and mix with wine. Bring up the heat
to sear the flesh. Watch how the nuggets of fat

render down. Good. Leave her to stew
in her own juice for half a day at least.

Now all that's left to do
is bring this dish to your dear: a single taste

and what you wish for most, that most
dangerous of wishes, will certainly come true.

JOHN FULLER

SORREL

Apologies to the snail
For gathering his dinner
    And perhaps tomorrow's,
With whom I have no quarrel
As fingers search for sorrel.

The leaves are stacked against
The thumb, ready to spring
    Apart again
As from the packed plastic
They dump their green elastic

And stir upon the table,
A dark dealt freshness,
    In gathered mounds
Of vegetable life
That moisten to the knife.

With butter in a pan
They fall to a khaki slime
    As sharp as a lemon.
Outside, it continues to rain
And the snails walk again.

FRANCES BISSELL

SORREL AND SNAILS

John Fuller's poem speaks to me on several levels. First, it immediately makes my mouth water, as in my mind I 'taste' the lemony sharpness of these floppy green leaves. Then, I have a cook's appreciation of his admirably accurate and succinct description of what happens to sorrel leaves, "with butter in a pan they fall to a khaki slime as sharp as a lemon." And as a writer of recipes I know that it would be impossible to express the process more elegantly. But, like the poet, I think of the snail. I love to forage for wild food — mushrooms, blackberries, samphire, fennel, cob nuts, crab apples, rocket, sorrel, herbs, horseradish — and I often wonder whose food supply I am trespassing on.

The poem also reminds me of the time I cooked snails, properly cooked snails, not simply opening a can. It reminds me of the kitchen, the garden, the people I cooked with, and the other recipes we cooked and shared.

My snail recipe really should begin 'first catch your snails'. For that is what we did in Jimena de la Frontera, in southern Spain where I taught some cookery courses. Up in the foothills of the Sierra Rondania, we felt far away from the Costa, the beaches and the sea, and wanted to eat rustic food. I had already ordered a rabbit from the local butcher, which, when I went to collect it, was much admired by the rest of the customers. With it, I planned to make a *paella del campo*, using rabbit, snails and vegetables, rather than the brightly coloured *paella* full of chicken, shellfish and red peppers that is more commonly served on the Costa.

Our hostess' housekeepers, identical twins Angeles and Carmen, have a wealth of knowledge about very local dishes, including snails in a spicy sauce, which they made for special occasions. They were not familiar with them as an ingredient for *paella*, although they acknowledged it was a good idea and offered to help me. Their advice was to collect them from the garden early in the morning, while it was still cool and damp, and place them in a container from which they could not escape. A Le Creuset casserole was perfect for the quantity we collected. The snails were sprinkled with a little flour, covered with the heavy lid, and left for about 48 hours.

Cleaning the snails is a laborious and not particularly pleasant process. Those of a sensitive disposition may like to skip the next part and simply open a can of snails if a *paella del campo* is wanted.

You will need plenty of salt for cleaning the snails. We had somewhat less than a kilo of snails, and used a similar amount of salt. Put them in a bowl and add the first batch of salt, using a handful at a time, and a couple of thick slices of lemon squeezed over the snails. Wearing rubber gloves, rub the snails between your hands in the salt, which will gradually draw out the slime. After 4 to 5 minutes, rinse, and drain the snails, rub with more salt and repeat the process until the water runs clear and is no longer thick. This will take about 40 minutes, and it is best to pour the rinsing water into a bucket, and throw it in the garden, or down a large outside drain, rather than down the sink. We used three buckets of water in preparing less than a kilo of snails. Snails done this way will not be part of a thirty minute dinner for six. On the other hand, you can use them in the *paella de campo* with a tasty wild rabbit, or you can prepare *caracoles in salsa picante*, a perfect *tapa* for 3 or 4 people. But first we cooked the snails.

Assuming you have up to a kilo of snails, cleaned as I have described, put them in a saucepan, cover with water and bring them slowly to the boil "when their little heads will appear", according to Angeles. Drain and rinse them with water, cover with fresh water, add two or three bay leaves, a generous sprig of mint, two dried chillies, half a teaspoon each of white and black peppercorns, cumin seeds, and dill seeds and a generous glass of *fino*. Simmer, uncovered, in this broth for at least an hour or so before adding them to the *paella*, or you can proceed with the spicy sauce recipe as follows:

SALSA PICANTE

In a frying pan, gently cook a peeled and sliced onion
in 3 tablespoons extra virgin olive oil until wilted.
Add a thick slice of 2-day old bread, broken into pieces,
a handful of shelled almonds, a couple of tablespoons of pine nuts,
and cook for a minute or two more.
Pound to a paste in a mortar or food processor.

Next, cook two large, ripe, chopped tomatoes and a green pepper,
not a hot one,
in three or four tablespoons extra virgin olive oil until soft,
and rub through a sieve.
Or blend until smooth.

Mix both parts of the sauce together,
and stir it into the pot of simmering snails.
The dish is ready when the liquid reduces
to the point where the sauce clings to the snail shells.
Serve hot, warm or cold.

Absolutely delicious with grilled chicken,
try this sauce too, as I did,
with fried rabbit liver and kidneys,
which I served as *tapas* before the *paella*.

JEANNE MACDONALD

DRESSED

Dad told me it was the kindest way,
so I brought it slowly to the boil
ignoring the tapping of bound claws.

When it had cooked I broke off the pincers
the eight spindly legs, easing the moist meat
from hip sockets. She was female:

under the flap that concealed her private parts
I uncovered inverted breasts. Pulling her body free
I discarded the dead man's fingers.

Beneath her eyes I located the stomach pouch,
gently removed it, not wanting the contents to spill
onto what fisher-wives claim is the tastiest.

Her inner frame was fragile, but I poked it with my skewer
the network of caverns split to reveal her white flesh.
I mixed the brown and white meat together, seasoned.

The shell washed, polished and refilled. The claws
on top as decoration. She was dressed: ready.

FRANCES BISSELL

TOMATOES

'Ode to the Tomato'
by Pablo Neruda

Reading this poem is like biting into a fragrant, sweet, ripe tomato, the juice bursting out of its tight skin, a thick skin which only comes with tomatoes grown outdoors. And the only seasoning required is right there in the poem, 'the filial essence of the olive tree', and salt.

The same simplicity is to be found in one of my favourite tomato recipes, which I have made my own over the years, cooking it for gala dinners in hotels and restaurants abroad, writing about it in books and newspaper columns and showing how to do it a cookery demonstrations. Jennifer Paterson described it 20 years ago in one of her *Spectator* columns, and she in turn had tasted it at a friend's house, so I do not know the exact origins of 'my' tomato pudding Constructed like a classic summer pudding, and with the taste and texture of the tomato sandwiches I remember from my childhood, this is a dish only to be attempted when you have the ripest, most flavoursome tomatoes.

This simple recipe works because of the pectin in tomatoes, which holds the pudding together without any need for gelatine, just as the pectin-rich redcurrants hold the summer pudding together. And it is deliciously fresh-tasting because the tomatoes are ripe, sweet and uncooked. For greatest effect, make it in a traditional pudding basin.

TOMATO PUDDING

Ingredients:
3 lb (1.5 kg) sweet ripe tomatoes
12–15 slices, medium thickness, firm white bread with the crusts removed
Coarse sea salt
Freshly ground black pepper

Extra virgin olive oil
Sherry vinegar

PEEL THE TOMATOES, and cut them in half. Scoop out the seeds, juice and pulp and process with the skins, and two or three whole tomatoes. Chop the remaining tomato flesh, and put it in a bowl. Rub the processed pulp, skins and extra tomatoes through the sieve to extract maximum juice and flavour. Taste the mixture, and then add just enough salt and pepper to season it and pour half of it over the chopped tomatoes.

Cut the bread into wedges, dip into the dressing, and line a large pudding basin, or small moulds if you prefer, to make individual puddings. Spoon in the chopped tomato, and cover with a round of bread. Cover the pudding/s, weight them, and refrigerate for six to eight hours or overnight. To serve, turn out on to a chilled plate, decorate with herbs, and serve with a tomato vinaigrette flavoured with sherry vinegar. Accompany with a salad of steamed baby artichokes, leeks, asparagus, broccoli spears, or other green summer vegetables.

LAWRENCE SAIL

Sᴘᴀʀʀᴏᴡɢʀᴀꜱꜱ

Butter-wet, lickerous,
tender tongue-tie,
wilt-headed fasces,
maytime mouth-melt,
work of our fingers,
lips and tongues,
more a bird
in hand than in the bush —
and giving us the way
to recover a baby's
unashamed delight,
afterwards, by sucking
each finger clean.

Tagliatelle with Fig and Chilli

11 oz (320g) Egg tagliatelle
8 Black figs
2 Dried chillies
2 Lemons
2 oz (50g) Parmesan
2 tbs Extra Virgin olive oil
3½ fl oz (100 ml) Double cream

Cut each fig into 8 pieces. Crumble the chilli. Grate the lemon peel of both lemons and squeeze the juice of one. Grate the Parmesan.

Bring a large pan of salted water to the boil and cook the tagliatelle until al dente.

While the tagliatelle is cooking, heat a frying pan large enough for the figs in one layer. Add the olive oil and when smoking, carefully place the figs in the pan turning them immediately to caramelise. Season and add the chilli.

Drain the pasta. Stir the lemon zest and juice into the cream and mix into the tagliatelle. Add the figs and serve with the Parmesan.

ALISON BRACKENBURY

Holiday

Christmas. I go back to bed with a fig
Whose belly is plump and swollen with seeds,
Crisp, gold as small fires, yet in each one
Is something dark and thick, which needs
To linger and be kept with care.
For the days are short, then the mornings start
Darker, as we freeze and work.
Earth fills the seeds at the lost fig's heart.

ANTONY WORRALL THOMPSON

BROWN SODA BREAD

Makes 2 loaves

1 ½ pints (900ml) milk
juice of 2 lemons
1 ¼ lbs (560g) brown whole meal stone ground flour
1 ¼ lbs (560g) plain white flour
2 rounded teaspoons salt
2 rounded teaspoons bicarbonate of soda

Preheat the oven to gas mark 8 (230° C, 450° F)

1. To sour the milk pour, into a large jug with in the lemon juice. Allow to stand 15 minutes to thicken before stirring.

2. Sieve the dry ingredients together in a large bowl. Make a well in the centre and add 1 ¼ pints (750ml) of the sour milk.

3. Working from the centre, combine the mixture with either your hand or a wooden spoon, adding more of the sour milk if necessary. The dough should be soft, but not sticky.

4. Turn out on to a floured board and knead lightly, just enough to shape into two round loafs. Flatten slightly to about 2 inches (5 cm) thick and place onto a sheet.

5. Using a large floured knife mark with a deep cross in each loaf and bake in the hot oven for 15–20 minutes, then reduce the heat to gas mark 6 (200° C, 400° F) for 20–25 minutes, or until the bread is cooked and loaves hollow when tapped. *Tip*: If preferred use prepared buttermilk instead of souring your own milk.

DENNIS O'DRISCOLL

MUSINGS ON BREAD AND POETRY

I've always assumed Seamus Heaney's great poem, 'Sunlight', to be a poem about making soda bread. When I was growing up — and even more so when he was growing up in an earlier generation — soda bread was the only kind of bread made in Irish houses. The poem refers to 'the scone rising'. Well, I'm sure his aunt in the poem wasn't making one small scone; she was baking a loaf of soda bread. Here's how the Shorter Oxford dictionary defines 'scone':

> "Orig., a large round cake made of wheat or barley-meal baked on a griddle; any of the quarters into which such a cake may often be cut. Now usu., a small sweet or savoury cake made of flour, milk, and a little fat, baked on a griddle or in an oven".

Heaney must mean the word in its original sense of large loaf — especially given that there were nine Heaney children to feed!

PAUL KITCHING

Juniper Restaurant

'WINTER PRESENTATION' OF SLOW BAKED BREAST OF DUCK SERVED PINK WITH PLUM PUDDING, ASSIETTE OF PEAR, BALSAMIC

Ingredients
1 trimmed, lean breast of duck, skinned
2oz (50g) plum pudding
4oz (100g) long grain rice

For the Pear Puree
8oz (200g) pears, cored, chopped but not peeled
4oz (100g) stock syrup
1 cinnamon stick

For The Sauce
2oz balsamic vinegar
½ pint (300ml) brown vegetable stock
1oz (25g) cream

1. PREPARE THE PEAR puree by putting the pears, stock syrup and cinnamon in a pan and poaching with the lid on for 40 minutes. Remove the cinnamon, blend and pass through a sieve. Leave to cool then funnel into a squeezy bottle.

2. Slow bake the duck breast for 40 minutes at 110° C (230° F). Remove and rest.

3. Whilst the duck is resting prepare the other ingredients. Warm the plum pudding by crushing with a fork, placing in a pan with the brown stock and gently heating.

4. Place the rice in a pan of cold water and lightly bring to the boil. Carefully simmer for five minutes, drain and refresh in cold water. Leave until dry to the touch then lightly sauté in olive oil.

5. To create the sauce reduce the balsamic vinegar by half and the vegetable stock by three-quarters. Mix together and add the cream but do not reheat.

6. Now slice the duck and arrange in a tower. Surround with the rice and place a dollop of pudding to one side, alongside a square of pear puree filled with the sauce.

MATTHEW WELTON

BUTTERNUTS

The girl who smelled like bubblegum admired the sky.
The telephone rang loudly. Moss grew on the roof.
The neighbours from across the lake would straggle by
for parties in the winter. Pairs of girls would goof

around the gardens where the paths were pebbled green.
The gummy girl would hardly talk. The night it rained
she danced a hula, fingering a tangerine.
She showed her teeth. *The sky is faultless*, she explained.

∾

The drunken uncles glooped around the garden-house
then went indoors and offered round their loose cigarettes
and hammered out some practice-piece and sang like cows.
The grey canary-gulls, they said, they kept as pets.

At night a smell like apricots would drowse the rooms.
But now the radio comes on and plays that march
with scrawly cellos, gasps of organ, piles of drums.
The trays of seedlings flourish in the kitchen-porch.

∾

All night they talked of breakfast. When the morning came
they cut the meat which tasted more like swedes or beer.
The bony man with monkey teeth was blue as blame,
as caned as custard, juiced as jellied eels. But here

the air takes on the taste of kaolin or yeast
or starch or lemon leaf. The evenings drop like plums.
As spruced as sprouts. As waxed as wasps. Completely spliced.
The breezes soften. Rain comes down. The heating hums.

~

The upstairs smelled of biro-ink. The kitchen smelled
like rained-on wool. The gardens smelled like boiling milk.
The wind that blew blew slowly and the circuits failed.
The rug was rashed with sun. The dark-faced girl would walk

about the bright and rainy streets. She peeled a pear.
The cousins in the kitchen played their reel of tape:
an hour's recorded silence. Shirts hung on a chair.
The sky was deep, and soft. The sky was chocolate soup.

~

The clouds collapse like coals. The sausage-dog that ate
the pears collapses by the trees, then comes inside.
The phone rang loudly. Papers blackened in the grate.
She answered, *Yes. A moment, please* — and walked outside

and swam around the lake. The gardens smelled like tin.
A smudge of sun, a whiff of wind; the rain that falls
falls early in the day. The afternoon wears in.
The shadow shifts in sheets, and daylight blues the walls.

STEAK AND KIDNEY PUDDING

A truly English dish, there is nothing like it in any other country's repertoire of receipts.

2½ oz (75g) beef dripping
1 large onion, chopped
35 oz (1 kg) Stewing steak, cubed
12 fl oz (350ml) beef stock
1 teaspoon mushroom ketchup
1 teaspoon Worcestershire sauce
1 teaspoon anchovy essence
1 lb (450g) ox kidney, core removed and cubed
7 fl oz (200 ml) red wine

for the pastry
10 oz (300g) self-raising flour
½ teaspoon salt
½ teaspoon white pepper
4 oz (120g) suet
iced water

Melt the dripping in a large flameproof casserole, add the onion and brown it in the fat. Remove the onion and set aside, then brown the steak in batches, then remove to rest with the onions. Pour off the fat from the casserole and put the pan back on the heat, adding the stock, mushroom ketchup, Worcestershire sauce, wine, and anchovy essence. Bring to a simmer, scraping up the bits in the pan. Return the onion and meat to the casserole and add the kidney. Cover the casserole and allow to barely simmer for about 1½ hours. When it is cooked, allow it to cool completely, preferably overnight.

Make the pastry at least 4 hours before you want to eat the pudding. Put the flour, salt, pepper and suet in a large basin and mix. Add enough iced water to make a soft, but not too floppy dough. Press it out into a large circle, cut a quarter section out and use the larger piece of dough to line a buttered 3½ pint (2 litre) pudding basin.

Fill the lined basin with the cold meat mixture, adding enough gravy to fill the bowl to within 1 inch (2 cm) of the top. Dampen the edges of the pastry and use the remaining pastry to cover the basin. Tie a sheet of buttered, pleated greaseproof paper over the top of the basin, then do the same with a piece of kitchen foil.

Fill a large pan with enough water to come at least half-way up the sides of the basin. Bring the water to a boil then lower the basin in, cover and keep the water at a rolling boil for about 10 minutes, then continue to cook for 2½ to 3 hours. Top the boiling water when necessary.

Remove the basin from the water, take off the papers, wrap a large white linen napkin around the basin, and spoon out the contents onto hot plates. Savour this with a glass or two of a handsome red Burgundy.

GILLIAN CLARKE

from FLESH

On its hook in the barn
The carcase is clean,
a licked bone from the sea.

He hands me two suet-caskets.
When I break them open,
With the whisper of tearing,

and hold in my hands the cold
soft weight of the kidneys before
slipping them from their silk,

they'll be the wet stones
of lamb's hooves,
the slippery ball of its head

in the birth-flood,
they will be the heart
of the new-born beating,

imagining the dead
in their cold places,
flesh in its fire and ice.

ANTONY WORRALL THOMPSON

TUSCAN-STYLE LAMB

2 lamb chump chops, fat and skin removed
4 garlic cloves, finely chopped
9 fresh tiny rosemary sprigs
1 tbsp extra virgin olive oil
1 onion, finely chopped
2 carrots, diced
2 celery sticks, diced
1 heaped tsp fresh thyme leaves
4 anchovy fillets, drained and finely chopped
1 glass red wine, about 4 fl oz (120 ml)
½ pint (300 ml) fresh lamb or chicken stock (from a carton is fine)
1 small can chopped tomatoes
1 tbsp tomato puree
14 oz (400g) can cannellini beans, drained and rinsed
2 tbsp chopped fresh flatleaf parsley
salt and freshly ground black pepper

SERVES 2

1. Toss the lamb chops with rosemary and half the garlic and season with pepper. Place in a non-metallic dish. Cover with plastic film and leave for 1 hour at room temperature or up to 24 hours in a fridge.

2. Heat a sauté pan. Spray with olive oil and fry the onion, carrots, celery and thyme over a high heat for about 10 minutes, stirring regularly until softened and lightly browned, then stir in the finely chopped garlic and anchovies.

3. Pour in the red wine, scraping the bottom of the pan with a wooden spoon to release any sediment, then add the stock, chopped tomatoes and tomato puree. Season, bring to the boil, then reduce the heat and simmer for another 15–20 minutes until well reduced and thickened, stirring occasionally.

4. Heat a griddle pan, barbecue or grill. Shake any excess oil from the chops and add to the pan of your choice. Cook for 5 minutes on each side until lightly charred and medium-rare. Season with salt.

5. Add the beans and most of the parsley to the tomato mixture and stir to combine. Season and cook for 5 minutes or until heated through. Spoon into wide-rimmed bowls, garnish with the rest of the parsley and arrange the lamb chops on top to serve.

MICHAEL SYMMONS ROBERTS

FOOD FOR RISEN BODIES – II

On that final night, his meal was formal:
lamb with bitter leaves of endive, chervil,
bread with olive oil and jars of wine.

Now on Tiberias' shores he grills
a carp and catfish breakfast on a charcoal fire.
This is not hunger, this is resurrection:

he eats because he can, and wants to
taste the scales, the moist flakes of the sea,
to rub the salt into his wounds.

MATTHEW FORT

FRICASSE OF PIG'S LIVER

21 oz (600g) pig's liver
3 ½ oz (100g) flour
1 tbsp Coleman's mustard powder
Salt & pepper
2 oz (50g) unsalted butter
2 tbsp peanut oil
10 fl oz (300ml) beer
Worcestershire sauce
1 tbs Dijon mustard

SERVES 4

Slice the liver into thin strips between 1 and 2 cm thick. Sift the flour and mustard powder salt & pepper into a big plate. Roll the strips of liver in the flour and mustard. In a large frying pan heat the butter and oil until smoking. Toss in the strips of liver (you may have to do this in several batches if your frying pan isn't big enough). Fry for 3 to 4 minutes, The strips should be crisp on the outside and pink within. Put them in a dish to keep warm. Pour any remaining fat out of the frying pan and pour the beer. Bring back to a seething boil and reduce by about 100ml. Take off the heat. Splash about 15 dashes of Worcestershire sauce into the liquid and stir in the mustard. Serve up the liver, pouring a little of the sauce.

LINDA FRANCE

THE MEAT FACTORY

The smell of raw meat is Chanel No.5.
It feels as if I'm right at home here
among the viscera, the flesh made new
and candy pink.
                        Dressed in disinfectant blue,
wellingtons, caps and rubber gloves, everyone
squelches on the tiled floor, stripping the willow
of troughs of offal to the dying chords
of the slaughterhouse next door.
                        Eggs are slotted
into the sockets of blushing, marbled pies.
Sausages are sleeved into cuff-linked lines.
Antique machines prick pat-a-cake pies,
six at a time for my baby and me.

Like summer rain, blood is never very far
away, the colour of the heart, the lights,
the sweet sweet breads.
                        Let me tell you, I've got the glad eye
for the boss of the chicken room, snowy with feathers
that tickle your gizzard, women cackling,
their fingers plucking. My skin is savoury
bumps.
                        Lunchtimes we go upstairs to the canteen,
carnal with smoke and greasy newsprint, and eat
anything at all with gravy, counting
the notes in our paypackets, already
twistin' the gnawed bone of Friday night away.

CLAIRE MACDONALD
Kinloch Lodge Hotel, Isle of Skye, Scotland

VENISON FILLET WITH WILD MUSHROOM SAUCE

Ingredients:
Trimmed venison fillet weighing 2 lb/900g
Olive oil, flaky salt, black pepper

For the sauce:
3 shallots — banana shallots, or 6 smaller ones, skinned and finely diced
4 tablespoons olive oil
2 lb (900 g) wild mushrooms, chopped — chanterelles are what we get most in our woods, but we have an excellent local grower of culti-vated wild mushrooms, so I could well include shitake and oyster in with my chanterelles
1 pint (570 ml) red wine, such as Merlot
½ pint (285 ml) double cream
Salt, pepper

SERVES 6

MAKE THE SAUCE by heating the olive oil in a sauté pan and sauté the finely diced shallots for two or three minutes. Scoop them into a warmed bowl and raise the heat in the sauté pan, and sauté the chopped wild mushrooms — you will need to do this in relays, so that the volume of mushrooms doesn't lower the heat in the pan, which then means that they release their juices and tend to stew rather than sauté. Cook them until they are very well done — as with cultivated mushrooms, this greatly enhances their flavours. As they cook, scoop them into a separate warm dish. You may need to use more olive oil during this cooking time than the recipe says. When the mushrooms are cooked, leave them in the bowl, but replace the sautéed shallots in the sauté pan, and add the wine. Simmer until the wine is reduced by about two thirds — the shallots absorb the flavour of the wine as it reduces. Then, replace the mushrooms in the pan, add the cream, taste and season with salt and pepper, and simmer gently until the sauce thickens.

To cook the venison – in a large sauté pan heat the olive oil with the flaky salt and a good grinding of black pepper. Don't season the meat itself as this encourages the juices to run from it. When the oil is very hot, seal the fillets well on all sides. This will give you meat which is underdone in the middle. If you would rather eat it more pink and less red, roast the seared fillets in a hot oven, gas mark 7 (420° F, 220° C), for 10 minutes. Leave the meat to rest (while you are at your first course) to let the juices settle, then slice, and serve with the wild mushroom sauce spooned around, or if you prefer, handed separately.

RUTH FAINLIGHT

LOVE-FEAST

Sulphur-yellow mushrooms like unlaid, unshelled eggs
inside a chicken's stomach when my mother cleaned it.
This morning, mushrooms on the lawn made me remember.

Bright as dew on the grass and silver with air-bubbles,
a stream of water splashed from the dull brass tap against
the side of the sink and over her red-chilled fingers when she
opened the carcass and laughed to show me how some were almost
ready — yolks only needing their coating of lime and mucus,
while others were still half formed, small as pearls or seeds.

Always, once the chicken was plucked and quartered and boiling
my mother would take those eggs, marked with twisting coils
of crimson threads like bloodshot eyes, and the liver put aside
on the draining-board in a chipped old china saucer, and fry them
with an onion to make our private treat. In the steamy
kitchen, the two of us would eat, and love each other.

DELIA SMITH

CHICKEN WITH SHERRY VINEGAR AND TARRAGON SAUCE

This is my adaptation of a classic French dish called *poulet au vinaigre*. It's very simple to make: the chicken is flavoured with tarragon leaves and simmered in a mixture of sherry vinegar and medium sherry without a lid, so that the liquid cooks down to a glossy, concentrated sauce. Serve with some well-chilled Fino sherry as an aperitif—perfect for a warm summery evening

1 × 3 ½ lb (1.75 kg) chicken, jointed into 8 pieces, or you could use 4 bone-in chicken breast portions
5 fl oz (150 ml) good quality sherry vinegar
15 fl oz (425 ml) medium-dry Amontillado sherry
12 shallots, peeled and left whole
4 cloves garlic, peeled and left whole
2 tablespoons olive oil
2 tablespoons fresh tarragon leaves
1 heaped tablespoon crème fraîche
salt and freshly milled black pepper

For the garnish:
8 small sprigs of fresh tarragon
You will also need a large, roomy frying-pan 9 inches (23 cm) in diameter.

SERVES 4

FIRST OF ALL heat the oil in the frying-pan and season the chicken joints with salt and pepper. Then, when the oil begins to shimmer, fry the chicken (in two batches) to brown well: remove the first batch to a plate while you tackle the second. Each joint needs to be a lovely golden-brown colour. When the second batch is ready, remove it to the plate to join the rest. Then add the shallots to the pan, brown these a little, and finally add the garlic cloves to colour slightly.

Now turn the heat down, return the chicken pieces to the pan, scatter the tarragon leaves all over, then pour in the vinegar and sherry. Let it all simmer for a bit, then turn the heat to a very low setting so that the whole thing barely bubbles for 45 minutes. Half-way through turn the chicken pieces over to allow the other sides to sit in the sauce. When they're ready, remove them to a warm serving-dish (right side up) along with the shallots and garlic. The sauce will by now have reduced and concentrated, so all you do is whisk the crème fraîche into it, taste and season as required, then pour the sauce all over the chicken and scatter with the sprigs of tarragon. This is lovely served with tiny new potatoes tossed in herbs and some fresh shelled peas.

IAN McMILLAN

YORKSHIRE PUDDING RULES

The tin must not gleam. Must never be new.
If there is dried sweat somewhere in its metal
It must be your mother's. The flour must be strong
And white as the face of Uncle Jack
When he came back from the desert. The eggs
Must come from an allotment. The allotment
Must belong to your father-in-law.
The eggs have to be broken
With one swift movement over the bowl.
If there is dried sweat somewhere in its Pyrex
It must be your mother's. The milk
Must have been delivered by Colin Leech
At 0430. The fork has to be an old one. The wrist
Must, simply must, ache after the mixing.
The flour must introduce itself to the yolk of the egg.
The egg has to be allowed to talk to the flour.
The milk must dance with them both: foxtrot, then quickstep.
The pepper must be scattered, black on off-white.
The oven must be hotter than ever.
The lard has to come in a tight white pack.
The lard must almost catch fire in the oven.
The oven door must open and you must shout
JESUS CHRIST as the heat smacks you in the chops.

Follow these rules
And the puddings will rise to heaven
And far beyond.

VIVEK SINGH

Cinnamon Club, London, England

TANDOORI BREAST OF SQUAB PIGEON

Pigeons get eaten throughout the subcontinent. One of my most memorable meals was in Bangladesh when I was visiting family as a teenager. We were waiting at a river crossing for a ferry to take us over and I wandered into a local restaurant (more of a roadside hut, if truth be told) where they had just shot and cooked some pigeons. My companions tried to drag me out of there, pointing out the unkempt kitchen conditions but I didn't care—they looked so delicious I had to try them. They were worth the week of dysentery I suffered as a consequence.

No such worries with Vivek's recipe, which uses most of the flesh on the squab but requires a friendly butcher to take the pain out of the preparation. The breast of the pigeon gets the tandoor treatment and the rest is minced into a stunning kebab. This is a user-friendly way of eating such a small bird that many are put off by because of dealing with the bones.

For the breasts:

1st MARINATION

2 pigeons, breasts de-boned but with the skin and the leg, liver and heart minced

1 teaspoon ginger paste

1 teaspoon garlic paste

1 teaspoon salt

1 teaspoon chilli powder

½ teaspoon lemon juice

2nd MARINATION

½ onion fried and blended into a paste

1 tablespoon yoghurt

½ teaspoon garam masala

½ teaspoon salt

1 tablespoon oil

For the kebabs:
1 tablespoon oil
¼ teaspoon royal cumin
1 finely chopped medium sized onion
¼ teaspoon chilli powder
¼ teaspoon ground roasted cumin
1 small beetroot boiled, peeled and finely chopped
½ inch (1 cm) of ginger, finely chopped
2 chopped green chillies
1 teaspoon salt
1 sprig of mint, shredded
¼ teaspoon garam masala
1 egg
Breadcrumbs

PAT DRY THE breasts and marinate with ginger paste, garlic paste, chilli powder, salt and lemon juice and leave for 20 minutes.

Sear them in a hot pan for two minutes either side, skin side first.

Then add the second marinade and finish at gas mark 7 (200° C, 400° F) in the oven for five minutes.

For the kebab:
Heat the oil in a pan, add the royal cumin seeds and when they crackle, add the chopped onions and sauté until golden brown. Add the minced pigeon and beetroot and sauté for three minutes, then add the red chilli powder and the cumin powder and cook further until the mixture is almost dry.

Add the ginger, green chilli, the mint and salt.

Allow the mixture to cool.

Shape the mince into four cakes. Dip them in an egg batter, then roll them in breadcrumbs and deep fry until golden brown and serve alongside the breast.

MATTHEW SWEENEY

CURRY

It smelt of curry,
the room smelt of curry,
but how? And why?
No cooker, no spices,
no Indian anywhere
near, no plates, forks,
spoons. But that yellow
there on the wall
was turmeric, and that
pod on the floor
was a cardamom.
Messy eaters, whoever
they were. And yes,
two empty beer bottles
in the bin, and crumbs
or shards of poppadom.
It made him hungry,
hungry for a curry.
They could have left
a portion of dhal,
a spoonful of spinach,
fifty grains of rice —
he could now make out
exactly what they'd had.
But where could he go
to obtain the same
or anything like it —
the airport? So how
had the smell got here?
He sucked it in,
muttering in Irish,

grabbed his red jacket,
vacated the flat
to go to a place where
a pizza came brazen
with chilli and garlic.

CYRUS TODIWALA

Café Spice Namasté, London

BADAAM KALI MURG

Ingredients:

For the stuffing:
1 lb (500 g) breast of chicken
3½ oz (100 g) paneer (indian whey cheese)
2 oz (50 g) raw whole almonds
3½ oz (100 g) chopped red onions
½ oz (10 g) green chilli
Salt as desired
3–4 tablespoons oil
Cocktail sticks
1 egg

For the gravy:
6 oz (175 g) chopped onions
½ teaspoon turmeric powder
1 teaspoon dhania powder
1 teaspoon chilli powder
7 oz (200 g) chopped tomato
2½ oz (75 g) almond powder
5 oz (150 g) yoghurt
Salt as desired
1 heaped tablespoon fresh chopped coriander
2 tablespoons oil

CLEAN AND TRIM the breast of chicken and place in the freezer on a tray until almost, but not quite, frozen. The idea of semi-freezing the meat is so that it can be sliced more easily without the fibres splitting.

Meanwhile, chop the whole almonds, very finely mince the red onion, crush the paneer with a fork to make a rough paste, and mince the green chilli (de-seed if you think it may be too hot). Add the ingredients for the stuffing in a small bowl and mix them well together. Season and set aside in the refrigerator.

Whilst the chicken is chilling in the freezer you can start with the preparations for the gravy. In a blender / liquidiser add the yoghurt, almond powder, turmeric, chilli & coriander powders and whip to a smooth paste. Add a little water, if desired, to bring the paste to the consistency of single cream. Finely chop the onions and chop the tomatoes.

Heat two tablespoons of oil in a small saucepan approximately 6 inches to 8 inches in diameter and sauté the onions. Stir regularly making sure not to leave any bits stuck to the edges. Do not allow browning or burning. For this ensure that the flame / heat is not too high. When the onions are pale add the chopped tomatoes and sauté for a minute or two. Now add the paste, a 100 ml of either water or light chicken stock, cover the pan and simmer.

When the chicken breast is firm but not frozen, remove from the freezer and cut into thin slices lengthways. Once you have got the slices, count them and divide the stuffing into the same portion size.

Beat the egg in a small bowl and, if you have a pastry brush, keep this ready. With the wider end of the breast slice away from you, line them out and brush with the beaten egg. Place an equal portion of the stuffing an inch from the bottom narrow end on each.

Spread the topping right across each end of that width and, taking the pointed end in first, make a roll. When each roll is complete, pierce with a cocktail stick so that the end does not open when sautéing. You may, if you like, cut the stick into two pieces and pierce one piece at either end of the roll.

Heat the oil in a frying pan and add the paupiettes or little rolls of stuffed chicken breast. Allow each side to brown a bit before turning them around so that they are evenly browned on all sides. You may not get a total evenness in browning simply because the protruding stick will not allow it to happen. However, do the best you can. Remove once sautéed on to a kitchen towel and dab off any excess fat. Add these to the gravy and simmer for a few minutes. Add the chopped coriander at the very last minute and remove from the heat.

Serve the rolls in a shallow platter and pour the sauce over them. Sprinkle with chopped nuts if you so desire or a little smattering of fresh cream. Serve with saffron flavoured pulao.

Note from the chef: This recipe is one of those that were poetically inspired during the Mughal Empire and the poetry of none other than Omar Khayyam.

SUBHADASSI

THE CHAPATTI TRICK

In the beginning was Vesta. Small packets
full of dubious matter to hydrate, boil,
mix together: extra chemistry lessons
on Sundays; my Mum's *one night off*.
Then onto the earth tottered Chicken Bhuna.
Friday night was a gallon of Tetley's,
Sher-e-Punjab by the Station. If provoked
—I often was—I performed The Chapatti Trick.
Now I play God on a weekend. Before starting
to cook I seed an Indian visualisation
to locate inspiration: is it Madras or Bengali:
Basmati or Idli? Grind my own spices,
oil my kharai: bring the matter in hand
to two mouths starved in the act of Creation.

Puddings

SELIMA HILL

Jam

I must have been about ten years old,
hiding in my place behind the sofa,

when suddenly I started saying *jam*,
and everytime I said it, it got bigger,

and seemed to glow, like apricots, or gold,
and then it grew a mouth, and called my name,

and when I heard it calling me like that
I felt what I would later know as *joy*,

and ran upstairs to be alone with it
and cradle its great head in my lap.

ROBERT SEATTER

MAKING LEMON CURD

I am making lemon curd
while you are travelling back to France.
(One o'clock you take the bus.)

An insanely domestic thing to be doing
in the middle of this black hole of loss;
but the precise imperatives
of the *Sainsbury's Cookbook of Afternoon Teas*
are a sort of comfort.
(Two o'clock you check in at Heathrow.)

Four brown eggs and four yellow lemons,
half a bag of caster sugar and half a pound of butter:
all you need for the perfect lemon curd.
(Three o'clock you fly to Lyon.)

Mix the sugar with the lemons,
and beat with patience for ten minutes or more
till you get a sticky paste that remains on the back
of a wooden spoon.
(Six o'clock your time you land, then
take a train to Montpellier.)

Then beat with more patience,
without letting the water boil
else it mars the smoothness of the curd.
Allow to cool and then place in the fridge.
(Ten o'clock you sleep alone in crisp white sheets,
in a foreign room, your mind still travelling.)

And I have a perfect lemon curd,
stoppered in a jar, labelled and dated
with the day that you left.

TONY SINGH

Oloroso Restaurant, Edinburgh, Scotland

LEMON & CRÈME FRAÎCHE MOUSSE

Ingredients:
6½ oz (190 g) crème fraîche
6½ oz (190 g) double cream
1¼ leaves of gelatine soaked in cold water
Zest of 1 lemon
Juice of ½ lemon
2 oz (50 g) castor sugar
½ vanilla pod, seeds scraped out

PLACE CRÈME FRAÎCHE, sugar and lemon zest in a bowl then mix thoroughly. Whip up the double cream to soft peaks and put to one side.

Place lemon juice in a small pan with an equal amount of water and warm.

Add the vanilla and gelatine, stir until it dissolves — make sure this mix never boils.

As soon as it has dissolved, beat it in to the crème fraîche mix, then fold in the cream. Leave it to set in the fridge.

JENNY HOPE

Fruit

You fed me. Firm lychees peeled
from goose-bumped flesh of sunset pink.
Figs divide and flower; four quarters; one whole.
Strawberry hearts bleed a head of seeds.

You split a peach. The soft kernel exposed.
On the table, the flushed cheeks of apples.
A pear hangs like a tear from the bowl;
its stem stronger than expected.

Note from chef Tony Singh: Here is one of my favourite food poems, by Jenny
Hope, and a recipe that goes well with it as you can change the garnish to the
sweetest fruit in season and the mousse lends its creamy sharpness to anything —
it's one of those things best shared with your special person.

MARY CONTINI

Director of Valvona & Crolla

COCONUT KISSES

You will need 6 ingredients:
5 oz (145 g) soft butter
3 oz (85 g) caster sugar
4 oz (110 g) plain flour and a little extra for dusting
2 oz (55 g) cornflour
2 oz (55 g) desiccated coconut
Some glacè cherries to decorate

and
Weighing scales
Small bowls and a large mixing bowl
Hand-held electric whisk
Sieve
Tablespoon
2 baking trays, greased and lined
Oven gloves and a timer
Spatula
Wire cooling rack

Turn on the oven to gas mark 4 (180° C, 350°F)

PUT THE SOFT butter and sugar into the large mixing bowl and beat
them with the hand-held electric mixer until the mixture is pale,
white and fluffy.

Sift the flour and cornflour into the bowl. Add the coconut strands.
Stir everything together with the tablespoon to make a dough. The
mixture is quite stiff. You might find it easier to dust your hands with
a little flour (clean hands, please) and press the mixture together by
hand.

Check that all the ingredients are in the mixture.

Take pieces of the mixture and roll them into little balls. Put them
onto the greased and lined baking tray. They will spread a little when
they cook, so space them well apart.

Push a glacè cherry into the middle of each coconut kiss, pressing it down with your finger.

Using your oven gloves, put the baking trays into the oven. Set the timer for 20 minutes.

The kisses are cooked when they just start to turn golden brown at the edges. Let them cool a little on the tray before using the spatula to transfer them to the wire rack.

Store them in a tight-lidded tin when they are cool.

They are especially nice to give as a present to someone you love!

Kiss. Kiss. Kiss.

PETER HOWARD

PANCAKE

Unpromising. Ingredients mixed to a glop
of anaemic paste. But somehow emerges the memory
of sunlight on wheat fields that danced
the wind's tune. Gold promises of egg
surprise it; together they greet the milk's slow
wealth. There's a spark like a wave's crest
whipped into spray urging them all
to celebration of themselves.
There's heat, older than you can imagine:
joy stored and matured for aeons,
and a suavity of oil to ease the eloquence.
The co-operation sizzles to a binding
vow of friendship. The dance invents
a juggler's dexterity, which pours out
so a wafer of done-to-a-turn batter is flipped
high with skilful flick, does the slow-motion
turn of a born acrobat, falls with precision,
connects again with the pan.
A whole kiss, an embrace of unalloyed devotion
and cooking to dappled brown on gold.
Here's lemon-juice, excited till it hurts;
a crackle of sweet grains to complement;
and the pancake's rolled reverently as a
religious scroll. The knife cuts, the
taste-buds scramble and strain, saliva urges,
and you can taste it before you can taste it,
at the point where anticipation and consummation meet.

William Sitwell, *editor of* Waitrose Food Illustrated, *submits a favourite recipe from one of his regular contributors accompanied by his grandfather's poem.*

FLOSSIE SQUIRES

BLACKBERRY AND APPLE CHARLOTTE

Preparation time: 20 minutes
Cooking time: 55 minutes

Ingredients:
2 large Bramley apples
caster sugar to taste
12 oz (350 g) blackberries
5 ½ oz (150 g) softened butter
6–8 medium-thick slices day-old white bread, crusts removed

SERVES 4

PEEL, CORE AND roughly chop the apples. Put in a large pan with one tablespoon water over a low heat. Cook for 10 minutes until the apples are soft, but not collapsed. Add sugar to taste, then add the blackberries, stir, and remove from the heat.

Preheat the oven to gas 4 (180°C, 350°F).

Butter the slices of bread well on one side. Use two thirds of them to line a one litre-capacity pie dish, placing them butter-side down and cutting to fit. Fill the dish with the blackberry and apple mix. Cut the remaining bread into rectangles and use to cover the filling, butter-side up. Sprinkle with more sugar.

Bake for 45 minutes or until golden and crisp. Serve immediately with cream or custard.

SACHEVERELL SITWELL

BLACKBERRYING

I am of a mind to go blackberrying
    which is a pity to do alone
One should always have companions for fruit-picking:–
So choose them carefully,
    there are the living to choose from,
Or you can choose them from the dead

It is a foraying into forgotten fields,
    some of them not seen for years on end,
And we could set forth in any of two or even three directions:–
    to the long spinney with a pond in the middle of it,
Or beyond that in the distance to the wood called Grumbler's Holt
    which means a bear had his lair there many hundred years
        ago,
A dead tramp was found in it some weeks back
    without his trousers,
And the police must draw their own conclusions;
    giving a feeling, even a meaning to the wood
Which in truth it had already,
    ever since I remember it

Or to the Armada Fields as we call them,
    beyond the old manor with that tell-tale date above the
        window:–
We choose the latter
    and soon begin to work along the hedges

To about where on that winter day,
    I so well remember,
While I was at work on *A Look at Sowerby's English Mushrooms
    and Fungi*,
    the giant dead puff-balls
Came tumbling, rolling towards us

like child-clowns in some nightmare circus,
Till they lodged just exactly here among these blackberries

Which do not compare to the more Northern blackberries of
        Foxton Wood,
    as a North Countryman myself I like to think:–
Childhood memories of which still work on me with a little
        tightening of the heart,
    and more still the taste of the little wild raspberries of the same
        wood
For the sharpness of their bite and rasp,
Of intent for whom? Surely of satyric,
    goat-haunch satisfaction and satiety,
I am thinking

It could be true that the further North you go
    the better are the wild berries,
Attaining to their best in Lapland and in Finland;
Always remembering that extraordinary breakfast at half-past six
        in the morning,
    at Bodo in Norway, just north of the Arctic Circle,
The dishes of unknown yellow or red berries
    with bowls of para-paradisal white, white milk;
Having flown past the Lofoten Islands lying off to the right,
    like an unimaginable, unattainable vision of Leonardo's,
Lasting out maybe for more than a hundred miles of ocean;
    and wondering what life could be like there;
Were there early frescoed churches as on the Aland Islands in the
        Baltic?
    There are certainly the wondrous wild flowers
And a peculiar breed of dog the Lofoten Seal Hound!
We had been to see two villages of Lapps,
    Kautokeini and Rovaniemi,
But only the Lappish women were there,
    the men had gone down to the sea with their reindeer herds;

We only saw the women and children and the huge dogs.
Yes! It was at Bodo where the Norweigan ex-naval officer
    of long experience in the Arctic
Came aboard the yacht to arrange the salmon fishing
    in the Alten-Fjord;
And walking with me in the town
    past a shop hung with huge polar bearskins that reached from
        floor
to ceiling

Told me he could never shoot another polar bear:—
    this was after he had watched one of them
At sight of a human being
Shamble away holding up a paw
    to hide the black patent-leather end to its nose,
The one patch of black in all the whiteness of the snow scene
    which made the bear vulnerable:—
I had never thought to find myself talking to someone
    with the knowledge of Nova Zembla and Spitzbergen

Blackberrying is maybe our nearest equvilalent
    to the *vendemmia* or grape-picking,
And hence the need for pleasing companions,
For Swanilda,
    with eyes I said like the auricula,
Embodiment of the pearlshell hour and first breath of morning;
Swanilda,
    who used to read my poems in the Tube,
Whom I apostrophised as Madonna of the Shoal of Pearls,
My memory of her is still inhabitant of the Madonna dell'Orto:—
    though dead these thirty years,
Now gone for ever into the lagoon of time

And we come down along one of the most far off, most distant of
      the hedges
   with a basketful of the most bacchic-looking of the
      blackberries,
Clusters that spill out their staining ichor
   so that it is like the slaughtered death bed of the berries,
So heavy the basket that we take it in turn to carry it,
   and it dyes even the dead leaves on the ground
If we put it down for a moment

FLEUR ADCOCK

Summer in Bucharest

We bought raspberries in the market;
but raspberries are discredited:

they sag in their bag, fermenting
into a froth of suspect juice.

And strawberries are seriously compromised:
a taint—you must have heard the stories.

As for redcurrants, well, they say
the only real redcurrants are dead.

(Don't you believe it: the fields are full of them,
swelling hopefully on their twigs,

and the dead ones weren't red anyway
but some mutation of black or white.)

We thought of choosing gooseberries,
until we heard they'd been infiltrated

by raspberries in gooseberry jackets.
You can't tell what to trust these days.

There are dates, they say, but they're imported;
and it's still too early for the grape harvest.

All we can do is wait and hope.
It's been a sour season for fruit.

PRUE LEITH OBE

MUSCOVADO HEAVEN

PUT SOME COMPOTE, jam, fruit or what have you in a shallow dish.

Stir equal parts double cream and plain yogurt together until gloopy-thick but not set.

Pour over the fruit.

Sprinkle really heavily with dark muscovado sugar (no other sugar will do!) and put in the fridge for half an hour or so. The sugar will dissolve into a dark lake.

If you like a bit of crunch sprinkle a little more sugar on top before serving. Or serve with a thin sweet biscuit.

Looks good in individual cocktail glasses too.

CAROL RUMENS

Recipes for Marriage

In the days when we made our own yoghurt,
Perpetual motion seemed within our power.
The recipe was simple, but it worked.

We stirred a few live drops, the 'natural' sort,
With scalded milk cooled in a glazed white jar,
In the days when we made our own yoghurt,

And set the oven low, a tick past *nought*.
Slowly it thickened, grew just nicely sour;
The recipe was simple, but it worked.

A fresh yeast odour always filled our flat.
One magic spoonful spawned a litre more,
In the days when we made our own yoghurt.

Yaorti me Meli was our just desert
At breakfast: honey made the desert flower!
The recipe was simple, and it worked.

Somehow, the bacillus died, the milk ran out,
There was less time . . . We use the local store
These days, and buy our Greek, or fat-free, yoghurt.
Friends still say we're the recipe that worked.

JANE DURAN

SNOW PUDDING

One way is to pour maple syrup
on fresh snow. Find a corner
by the house that the wind misses.
Do not dream of it but do it —
syrup that drifts from the maple,
your sticky mittens.

Or sprinkle gelatine over water,
add sugar, lemon. Heat gently.
It seems so effortless
like the minnows that will appear
in the pond this summer,
so many tourings against rock,

remedies, quickenings
or the powerful states of shade
under the waterfall.
Beat the egg whites — fold in
to bring the snow that races,
the doe at the window.

In grandmother's kitchen
there is an ooze from the oven dish
with the Atlantic in it,
a hush over it,
an invisible recipe
at the back of the cookbook —

how to prepare snow
when it is really taking you sideways
out of control —
past the side of the house
past the lost barn, journeying
with the blurred crossings

everywhere the land still rising.
Bring in your black and white branches.
Lay your icy clouds on the table.
The roads are impassable.

IAN McKERRACHER
Landlord, The Helyar Arms, East Coker, Somerset, England

VALRHONA CHOCOLATE PUDDING

Ingredients:
8 oz (240 g) Valrhona dark chocolate
8 oz (240 g) unsalted butter, plus butter for greasing
6 eggs
4 egg yolks
4½ oz (130 g) caster sugar
6½ oz (180 g) plain flour
Cocoa powder

BUTTER 10 RAMEKIN dishes. Coat with cocoa powder, shaking off the excess.

Break the chocolate and cut the butter into small pieces, put them into a bain marie (water bath) and melt over a low heat.

You will need a food processor for the next stage. In the food processor mixing bowl, combine the eggs, additional egg yolks and caster sugar. Whisk at high speed for several minutes until the mixture is light and fluffy. Add the flour, using a metal spoon. Fold it in gently. Then gradually add the melted chocolate and butter, again handling the mixture gently to avoid breaking the air bubbles.

Divide the mixture between the ramekin dishes. Bake on a tray in a hot oven for eight minutes (or nine minutes if you have made the mixture in advance and held it in a refrigerator).

To serve, slide a knife round the pudding to loosen it. Up-end the ramekin over a plate and give the pudding a gentle shake to release it. Serve with a spoonful of clotted cream or vanilla ice cream.

Timing is critical. The pudding should be very gooey inside and when you put your spoon into it, the centre should ooze out. The only way to get this right is trial and error!

JANE ROUTH

A SUMMER PUDDING

I didn't have time to pick redcurrants and raspberries
for the summer pudding I was making for tea

because I had to wash and change my clothes
after I'd slipped on a pile of goose shit
when I was trying to catch a young gander
who ran up and down the wrong side of the fence
without the sense to fly back to the flock
when he landed in the windrowed hay
after they'd all taken off in fright at a snake
that was only a hosepipe I'd laid from the house
to buckets by the gate because the troughs wouldn't fill
since I'd turned off the stopcock in the field
after the barn started to flood when the Belfast sink
fell to the floor and pulled water pipes out of the wall
because the tractor rammed it at full speed as you-know-who
hadn't been quick enough to turn out through the doors
when he knocked the throttle on full waving his arms
because a wasp was cruising around and he can't stand
dirt rats ants flies mosquitoes or bees,
always wears gloves and is squeamish:

I was just slicing the bread to line out the bowl
when he came for the tractor key. Would you like toast?

Note from the author: The food poem I always refer to this time of year is by
Grevel Lindop — it's in his *Collected* from Carcanet (2002) — simply called
'Summer Pudding'.

Yes, I use it AS a recipe — makes a much better summer pudding than all my
recipe books. It opens:

> "Begin with half a pound of raspberries
> picked from the deep end of your sloping garden, where the birds

play havoc with the draggled fruitnets
                . . ."

but the best bit is his suggestions of how to eat it:
    ". . . let it be on one of three
        occasions; for a kitchenful of children
    whose mouths grow purpleringed and flecked with
        whipped cream as they dig
    and lose, entranced, the treasure of the minute;
        or for the friends around your polished table, when that soft
    lake of mahogany reflects the faces
        melting in candlelight and burgundy, rivers of talk
    eddying to a stillness lost in taste
        . . ."

Oh, and his poem gets a ceremonial reading before the pudding is eaten!

Very Best Chocolate Cake

A cake made in the processor or mixing machine and therefore very easy—a deliciously naughty icing too!

Ingredients:
2 oz (50 g) cocoa
6 tablespoons boiling water
3 eggs
2 fl oz (60 ml) milk
6 oz (175 g) self-raising flour
1 rounded teaspoon baking powder
4 oz (100 g) soft butter
10 oz (275 g) natural caster sugar

For the icing and filling:
5 oz (125 g) Bournville chocolate broken into small pieces
5 fl oz pouring double cream
3 tablespoons apricot jam

Pre-heat the oven to gas mark 4 (180° C, 350° F)
Grease two 8 inch (20 cm) sandwich tins and base line with baking parchment.

First process the cocoa and boiling water until well mixed. Add the remaining ingredients to the processor and whiz for one-two minutes, scraping down the inside of the bowl if necessary. The mixture will be a thickish batter (be careful not to over-whisk). Divide the cake mixture between the prepared tins. Bake in the pre-heated oven for about 25–30 minutes until well risen and shrinking away from the sides of the tin.

For the icing and filling, measure the chocolate and cream together in a bowl and stand the bowl over a pan of simmering water for approx 10 minutes until melted—stirring from time to time. Set aside and allow to become cold and almost set.

When baked, remove the cakes and allow to cool completely. Spread the tops of each cake with apricot jam. Fill the cakes with half the icing and spread the remainder on top. Take a small palette knife and draw large "S" shapes to give a swirl effect—dust with icing sugar and enjoy!

HENRY SHUKMAN

A GLASS OF GUINNESS

Standing in the kitchen with a Guinness
in one hand and a steaming plate of tagliatelle
in the other, I thought: wine with pasta.
But I was thirsty, and threw it all but down
in a single pouring of cream, and let out an *ah*,
and for a moment was back
                            in my mother's kitchen,
a summer morning flickering through leaves outside,
and in my hand the thick glass pitcher that attached
to the Kenwood, full of a milkshake's icy cement
freshly mixed by me. The aroma of chocolate
and vanilla filled my head, and faintly too
the smell of the mixer's hot electrics.
And there was something else so rich, so sweet,
such a thickness in the air it left me reeling.

ELIZABETH SMITHER

THREE WOMEN SHARING A BOWL OF CRÈME BRÛLÉE

In a small brown pudding bowl
with a syrup-coloured stripe
on a brown base plate

our three spoons scoop.
'One *crème brûlée, s'il vous plaît*
and three dining-with-the-devil spoons.'

One indivisible glacé cherry
at the centre like a navel
how unsophisticated in a sophisticated

restaurant to have just one
surviving appetite after the appetiser
a glass of house white

and two compatriots press-ganged
into something they've never conceived:
burnt cream. Culinary accidents

the culinary leader speaks of
that upended tart with apples
dropped on the hot plate by a furious

overheated woman named Tatin
or crêpes Suzette accidentally designed
by someone half-pickled

accidents which on the instant of occurring
or in culinary terms – combining – become
a poet's inspired instinctive metre

a villanelle perhaps, an enjambment
so full of joy its creation
resembles wind through the open window.

'Satisfactory?' The waiter goes past
peers in the bowl where spoons
keep returning over faint protests

'I'm not really hungry but I can't resist.'
'You have the cherry. It was your idea.'
And as the last crumbs of the crust

are tenderly scraped we seem to be
wrapping the crying Tatin in a shawl
and setting her in a rocker, bringing brandy

or toasting crêpes Suzette with more brandy
deliriously clinking glasses until we swoon
over the tablecloth in huge top-heavy hats.

CRÈME BRÛLÉE

You can make individual crèmes, or one large, shallow dish, which gives you just the right amount of crème to brûlée.

18 fl oz (500 ml) cream
6 egg yolks
2 oz (50g) vanilla sugar

Put the cream into a saucepan and heat gently to simmering point. Beat the egg yolks and vanilla sugar in a large bowl until well amalgamated. Pour the hot cream onto the egg mixture, stirring it vigorously. Pour through a fine strainer into a shallow gratin dish (or individual ramekins) and place in a baking tin of boiling water. Put into a medium hot – about 140° C (285° F) – oven for 45 minutes. Remove and allow to cool, then chill. About 1 hour before serving, dredge a fine layer of caster sugar over the top and flame it with a blowtorch until you have a nice, brown crisp caramel top.

BEN JONSON

To Penshurst *(an extract)*

Then hath thy orchard fruit, thy garden flowers,
Fresh as the ayre, and new as are the hours.
The earely cherry, with the later plum,
Fig, grape, and quince, each in his time doth come:
The blushing apricot, and woolly peach
Hang on thy walls, that every child may reach . . .
And no-one empty-handed, to salute
Thy lord, and lady, though they have no sute.
Some bring a capon, some a rural cake,
Some nuts, some apples; some that think they make
The better cheeses, bring 'hem; or else send
By their ripe daughters, whom they would commend
This way to husbands; and whose baskets beare
An emblem of themselves, in plum or peare.
But what can this (more than expresse their love)
Add to thy free provisions, farre above
The need of such? Whose liberall boord doth flow,
With all, that hospitalitie doth know! . . .
Here no man tells my cups; nor, standing by,
A waiter, doth my gluttony envy:
But gives me what I call, and lets me eate,
He knowes, below, he shall finde plentie of meate,
Thy tables hoord not up for the next day,
Nor, when I take my lodging, need I pray
For fire or lights, or liverie: all is there;
As if thou, then, wert mine, or I reign'd here . . .

This poem was recommended by poet John Mole as one of his personal
favourites.

National Poetry Day menu

JOHN KEATS

from THE EVE OF ST. AGNES

And still she slept an azure-lidded sleep,
In blanched linen, smooth, and lavendered,
While he from forth the closet brought a heap
Of candied apple, quince, and plum, and gourd;
With jellies soother than the creamy curd,
And lucent syrops, tinct with cinnamon;
Manna and dates, in argosy transferred
From Fez; and spiced dainties, every one,
From silken Samarkand to cedared Lebanon.
These delicates he heaped with glowing hand
On golden dishes and in baskets bright
Of wreathed silver: sumptuous they stand
In the retired quiet of the night,
Filling the chilly room with perfume light. –
"And now, my love, my seraph fair, awake!
"Thou art my heaven, and I thine eremite:
"Open thine eyes, for meek St. Agnes' sake,
"Or I shall drowse beside thee, so my soul doth ache."

Note from Geoff Pick of Keats House: One of the sources for the poem was the
popular belief that, on the Eve of St. Agnes, a girl could make her future husband
appear to her in a dream where they would kiss and feast together. Porphyro lays
out this (real) feast for his love Madeline in the hope that she will wake and fall
in love with him.

FANNY KEATS

This recipe was donated by Keats House

FANNY KEATS'S PLUM CAKE

Ingredients:
1 lb (450 g) brown breadcrumbs
1 lb (450 g) raisins
½ lb (225 g) currants
A little flour
3 oz (85 g) candied peel
½ lb (225 g) sugar
1 lb (450 g) butter
4 eggs
4 egg whites
6 fl oz (175 ml) rum
4 fl oz (110 ml) milk (approx)
1 teaspoon grated nutmeg
Grated rind of ½ lemon

PUT THE DRIED fruit and peel into a bowl and sprinkle with the flour
and nutmeg. Mix to coat and separate the fruit. Cream the butter
and sugar, beat in eggs with lemon rind. Gradually add the fruit and
breadcrumbs, beating well, adding the rum and enough milk to bind.
Turn into a lined, greased 8 inch (20 cm) cake tin and bake in oven
at gas mark 2 (150° C, 300° F) for 3½–4 hours. Cover with foil or
greaseproof paper after two hours to prevent over-browning.

FANNY KEATS

This recipe was donated by Keats House

FANNY KEATS'S HAZELNUT OR WALNUT CAKE

Ingredients:
6 oz (160 g) sugar
3 eggs
¼ pt (140 ml) milk (approx.)
4 oz (100 g) chopped nuts
4 oz (100 g) brown breadcrumbs

BEAT THE EGGS with the sugar until smooth, pale and fluffy. Fold in the nuts and breadcrumbs and enough milk to give a dropping consistency. Turn into a greased 7 inch cake tin and bake for 15 minutes in oven at gas mark 7 (425° F, 220° C), then reduce temperature to gas mark 4 (350° F, 180° C) and cook for 20–30 minutes until cake is firm to touch.

FRANCES MARY (FANNY) KEATS (1803–1889) was the only sister of the poet John Keats. After her mother's death in 1810, she lived with her grandmother Mrs Jennings in Edmonton, Middlesex, now North London. On the death of Mrs Jennings in 1815, she went to live with her guardians Mr and Mrs Richard Abbey, in Walthamstow in Essex, until she came of age in 1824.

Tradition has it that these recipes came from Mrs Jennings, who was known to be a good cook. According to Fanny Keats's descendants, these two recipes were taken by Fanny when she left England for Spain with her Spanish husband, the novelist Valentin Llanos y Gutierrez, in 1833. The recipes were translated into Spanish, presumably for their cook, and were translated back into English in the 1930s.

The plum cake is a traditional 'Twelfth-Day Cake' made to be eaten on Twelfth Night, the final day of the Christmas festivities. The nut cake can also be used as a filling for a pastry case, like a Bakewell tart.

JULIA BIRD
Poetry Book Society

HONEY BUNS WITH SULTANAS

Ingredients:
3 oz (85 g) butter
3 oz (85 g) set honey
1 beaten egg
2 ½ oz (70 g) sultanas
8 oz (250 g) self-raising flour
A little milk

MAKES 12

FIRST CREAM TOGETHER the butter and honey to a consistent texture. Next add the egg, beating it in smoothly, little by little. Then add the sultanas and stir in the flour. Add enough milk to give the mixture a dropping consistency. Grease a bun tin thoroughly, and spoon in the mixture to half-fill the tin. Bake at gas mark 5 (375° F, 190° C) for about 15 minutes.

To be eaten with 'Bee Lines' by Jamie McKendrick.

Inspired by a recipe on the *Green Chronicle* website: www.greenchronicle.co.uk

JAMIE MCKENDRICK

BEE LINES

The novice keepers, togged in gloves and goggles,
smoked out the spirit of the hive and laid
three trays, each caked with hexagons,
on the oak table where they sat and ogled
the gold light trapped in the grid of cells
till their lids grew heavy and they trudged to bed.

Lying beside her husband, she wasn't sure
if she was the burglar or the burgled
caught napping as the whole place was stripped bare
but she dreamed herself on the crest of an elm
where a swarm was scouring half an eggshell
whilst the piping of the queen bestrode the air

dainty as a sea-chest in a maelstrom.
She woke to find a double stream
of bees, one coming down, the other climbing
the chimney, heaving bags of it back to the hive,
and when the last ingot had taken wing
the hearthstone was backlit like the gate of heaven.

KEITH RUTTER
Orange Studio Restaurant, Birmingham, England

In an event celebrating National Poetry Day, each course is announced with poetry written for the occasion, the flavours of the food being matched by the flavours of the poems. Roz Goddard is Birmingham Poet Laureate 2003–2004. Richard Grant is one of our feistiest performance poets and a dab hand in the kitchen too!

MENU

Cauliflower & sorrel soup
Garlic tartines with grilled scallops & crispy bacon
Crushed goats cheese with pepper & black cherry jam

Duck with balsamic cherries and shiitake mushrooms
Nutmeg and cream cheese tart served with minted jus
Lamb noisettes with basil & parmesan crust

Potatoes with garlic, lemon & walnuts
Roasted baby carrots with cumin
Fine beans with shallots & basil

Tangy lemon tart with a raspberry cream
Saffron pavlova with lime curd

(This menu was commissioned for the 2004 Orange Birmingham Book Festival)

DREADLOCK ALIEN AKA RICHARD GRANT

"Okay, tonight's menu includes some of the chef's personal favourites
and a signature dish or two. My job as the word waiter is to
collectively entice, excite and then sell, sell, sell, them to you.

≈

For starters we have a medley of metaphors, pan fried with a prose
pourri, layed upon a bed of books and drizzled with a story and
stanza sauce.

≈

Followed by a sharp yet subtley sweet, sorbet burst of simillie and
sentence.

≈

For main course we have oven roasted rhyme, toasted thyme and
money glaze.

≈

For vegetarians we have a verb and vowel vol ou vent, stacked on a
published pastry case, laced with a lingo & slang meringue.

≈

Main course is served with lashings of poetry mash, and a panache of
garden verb vegetables.

≈

For dessert we have a choice of fresh phrase salad and double
couplet cream
or
Dub Poetry Ghetto, with colloquial essence and fresh whipped words

∽

Finish with a cup of freshly noun ground novel beans
Served with fresh mint messages and praline snaps.

∽

Warning some of the above dishes may contain traces of thought and
message."

(This poem was commissioned for the 2004 Orange Birmingham Book Festival)

ROZ GODDARD

THE CHEF'S EYES

It's like being on the Pepsi Max,
every day a fresh ride.
I didn't know food could be this exciting
When we see a barrel of sardines, silver
and glittering, his skin changes temperature
heart climbs another step. He plunges in
brings out handfuls that tumble
through his fingers like rain.

The market is the place for romance,
we fall in love twenty times a day
Pomegranates blush just for us
shy apples roll away, nestle beside onions.
Bread rises up on stall after stall like clouds
fallen to ground.

Sometimes I think he will cry when he inspects
a rib-eye steak, the fine lines of ivory,
ruby flesh. He murmurs to himself
like a painter who has found the right colour—
lemon and saffron delight him
lime is his lucky mascot.

When the pans and skillets are quiet,
the empty dining chairs still against the wall
he breakfasts at midnight on bronze tea
eats black pudding marbled with a universe of stars
is astonished at all he has left to taste.

(This poem was commissioned for the 2004 Orange Birmingham Book Festival)

JULES MANN
The Poetry Society

VEGETARIAN SUN-DRIED TOMATO AND AUBERGINE LASAGNE

Best made with fresh pasta, this dish requires a meditative amount of time to prepare, but that's all part of the savouring.

Pasta:
2 cups (8 oz / 250 g) flour
2 eggs
1 tablespoon olive oil, and/or water as needed
2 tablespoons fresh basil, chopped finely
Freshly ground black pepper
Pasta machine (flat lasagne noodle setting)

Tomato Sauce:
2 cups (14 oz / 400 g) of fresh or canned tomato puree
½ cup (1 oz / 25 g) sundried tomatoes, reconstituted (let sit in hot water for 5 minutes, remove and chop finely)
4 shallots, finely chopped
Olive oil

Cheese and Basil:
Buffalo mozzarella, or fresh mozzarella
30 or so large fresh leaves of basil, washed

Roasted Garlic:
2 heads of garlic
Olive oil
Thyme branches
¾ cup (5 oz / 150 g) cottage cheese

Aubergine:
1 large or 2 small aubergines
Olive oil

PREPARE THE LAYERS first, then assemble the lasagne.

Roasted Garlic: combine all ingredients except the cottage cheese in a glass or heavy-bottomed roasting pan; roast in a low oven (gas mark 2, 300 ° F, 150° C) for 1½ hours or until garlic heads are very soft and slightly caramelised. When done, ease out of the papery skin and mash the soft heads into the cottage cheese.

Aubergine: slice in ¼ inch rounds, lay out in a non-stick (or foil-lined) roasting pan, sprinkle with a bit of olive oil, cover with foil and put in the oven at the same time as the garlic until soft (it shouldn't take so long to get soft — check after 45 minutes).

Pasta: lightly whisk eggs, put flour in bowl, hollow out the middle and pour egg mixture in, stir with wooden spoon and then knead with hands. If more liquid is needed, use olive oil and/or water. Knead until everything sticks together loosely, then grab ⅓ of it at a time to knead in both hands for five minutes, until it feels malleable and smooth. Pat down into a hamburger shape. When done, wrap each one individually in plastic or butcher paper and refrigerate for at least half an hour, allowing the dough to rest. Half an hour before you're ready to assemble the lasagne, bring it out of the refrigerator, give it five minutes or so and then run through the pasta machine until the sheets are as thin as possible without holes (careful — the fresh herbs and black pepper can cause it to tear more easily). Hang up to dry.

Tomato Sauce:
Heat the olive oil in a saucepan, add shallots and cook for five minutes on low heat until soft; add the sundried and tomato purée, leave on low heat for at least 15 minutes to enhance the flavour. Set aside to cool.

Cheese and Basil:
Slice cheese thinly, set aside with basil leaves.

Lasagne Assembly:

Gather all components into your immediate work area. Oil bottom of glass baking pan (olive oil preferred). A suggested order of layering follows, but feel free to create your own pattern; when layering the pasta, overlap the edges slightly; they should run up but not over the sides of the pan:

Thin layer of tomato sauce / pasta / roasted garlic mixture / tomato sauce / pasta / buffalo mozzarella / basil leaves / pasta / roasted garlic mixture / aubergines / tomato sauce / pasta / buffalo mozzarella / basil leaves / pasta / tomato sauce.

Bake at gas mark 5 (375° F, 190° C) for 35 minutes (if using fresh pasta — another 10 minutes or so if not). Let it sit for five minutes before cutting. Lasagne typically tastes even better the next day, if you can refrain from finishing it all in one go. Or, make it ahead of time, cook it and freeze it — it reheats beautifully.

This is particularly tasty with a salad of rocket and fresh English peas . . . and a California Zinfandel!

ROGER McGOUGH

VEGETARIANS

Vegetarians are cruel, unthinking people.
Everybody knows that a carrot screams when grated.
That a peach bleeds when torn apart.
Do you believe an orange insensitive
to thumbs gouging out its flesh?
That tomatoes spill their brains painlessly?
Potatoes, skinned alive and boiled,
the soil's little lobsters.
Don't tell me it doesn't hurt
when peas are ripped from the scrotum,
the hide flayed off sprouts,
cabbage shredded, onions beheaded.

Throw in the trowel
and lay down the hoe.
Mow no more
Let my people go!

ROGER McGOUGH

THERE WAS A KNOCK ON THE DOOR.
IT WAS THE MEAT

There was a knock on the door.
It was the meat. I let it in.
Something freshly slaughtered
Dragged itself into the hall.

Into the living-room it crawled.
I followed. Though headless,
It headed for the kitchen
As if following a scent.

Straight to the oven it went
And lay there. Oozing softly to itself.
Though moved, I moved inside
And opened wide the door.

I switched to Gas Mark Four.
Set the timer. And grasping
The visitor by a stump
Humped it home and dry.

Did I detect a gentle sigh?
A thank you? The thought that I
Had helped a thing in need
Cheered me as I turned up the heat.

Two hours later the bell rang
It was the meat.

INDEX OF POEMS AND RECIPES WITH ACKNOWLEDGMENTS

Salt Publishing is grateful to the contributors and publishers listed below for their permission to print material in this anthology. Every effort has been made to trace the copyright holders. If any material has been included without appropriate acknowledgement, Salt Publishing would be glad to hear from the copyright holder.

McGough, Roger: 'There was a Knock on the Door. It Was the Meat.' p 127 (from *Collected*, Penguin 2003), selected by the Poetry Society

McGough, Roger: 'Vegetarians' p 126 (from *Collected*, Penguin 2003), selected by the Poetry Society

McKendrick, Jamie: 'Bee Lines' p 118 (from *Ink Stone*, Faber & Faber 2003), selected by the Poetry Book Society

McKerracher, Ian: 'Valrhona Chocolate Pudding' p 103 (The Helyar Arms, East Coker, Somerset)

McMillan, Ian: 'Yorkshire Pudding Rules' p 76, copyright Ian McMillan (www.ian-mcmillan.co.uk), written for The Poetry Society's *Poetry On A Plate* book for National Poetry Day, 7 Oct '04 (Enquiries adrian@uktouring.org.uk Tel/fax +44 (0)1684 540366)

Melchioretto, Valeria: 'Bridging Gaps Between Blackboards' p 12

Mole, John: 'The Banquet' p 24

Murphy, Michael: 'Ovid in an English Kitchen' p 23 (*Elsewhere*, Shoestring Press 2003)

Neruda, Pablo: 'Ode to the Onion' p 13, 32 and 'Ode to the Tomato' p 48 (*Fifty Odes*, translated by George Schade, Host Publications 2001, also in *Elemental Odes*, translated by Margaret Sayers Peden, Libris, 1991)

Parkes, Nii Ayikwei: 'Deep Fried Yam with Avocado Kpakpo Shito' p 10

Popa, Vasko: 'St. Sava's School' p 14 (from *Collected Poems*, Anvil 1997)

Ritchie, Sue: 'Chilled Beetroot and Apple Soup' p 16

Robb, Rachel: 'Baked Halloumi with Puy Lentils and Tomato Sauce' p 19

Robb, Rachel: 'Spicy Caramelized Red Onion Soup' p 18

Roberts, Michael Symmons: 'Food for Risen Bodies – II' p (from *Corpus*, Cape 2004)

Rollinson, Neil: 'Onions' p 33

Routh, Jane: 'A Summer Pudding' p 84 (with reference to 'Summer Pudding' by Grevel Lindop from his *Collected*, Carcanet 2002)

Rumens, Carol: 'Recipes for Marriage' p 80

Rutter, Keith: 'Menu' p 97 (commissioned by Book Communications for the Orange Birmingham Book Festival 2004)

Sail, Lawrence: 'Sparrowgrass' p 50

Seatter, Robert: 'Making Lemon Curd' p 67 (from *Travelling to the Fish Orchards*, Seren 2002)

Sheers, Owen: 'Hedge School' p (commissioned by The Poetry Society during a residency at Heston Blumenthal's restaurant, The Fat Duck, for National Poetry Day 2004)

Shukman, Henry: 'A Glass of Guinness' p 88

Singh, Tony: 'Lemon & Crème Fraîche Mousse' p 68 (Oloroso Restaurant, Edinburgh)

Singh, Vivek: 'Tandoori Breast of Squab Pigeon' p 57 (Cinnamon Club, London)

Sissay, Lemn: 'Sandwich Love' p 39 (from *Morning Breaks in the Elevator*,

Payback Press 1999)

Sitwell, Sacheverell: 'Blackberrying' p 74 selected by William Sitwell, editor of *Waitrose Food Illustrated* (from *An Indian Summer*, Macmillan 1982)

Smith, Delia: 'Chicken with Sherry Vinegar and Tarragon Sauce' p 54, copyright © Delia Smith 1993 — Recipe reproduced by permission from *Delia's Summer Collection* (Published by BBC Worldwide). Acknowledgements also to one of the Poetry Society's 2004 NPD poet in residence host organisations, FARMA (National Farmers' Retail & Markets Association), of which Delia Smith is a patron.

Smith, Simon (Translator): 'On Drinking Your Good Health' p 22, by Horace (*Odes* Book 1.20)

Smither, Elizabeth: 'Three women sharing a bowl of crème brûlée' p (from *A Question of Gravity*, Arc Publications 2004)

Squires, Flossie: 'Blackberry and Apple Charlotte' p 73 (as published in *Waitrose Food Illustrated*)

Subhadassi: 'The Chapatti Trick' p 64 (from *Peeled*, Arc Press 2004)

Sweeney, Matthew: 'Curry' p 59

Sweeney, Matthew: 'Egg' p 4

Sweeney, Matthew: 'Salata de Vinete' p 3, or Aubergine Salad

Swift, Jonathan: 'Onyons' p 31

Tate, James: 'Soup of Venus' p 13 (from *Selected Poems*, Wesleyan University Press 1991)

Todiwala, Cyrus: 'Badaam Kali Murg' p 61 (Café Spice Namasté)

Wardle, Sarah: 'Word Tasting' p 28 (from *Fields Away*, Bloodaxe 2003)

Williams, Frances: 'Oyster Eating' p 26 (from *Wild Blue*, Seren 2000)

York, Jessica: 'Apricot and Almond Crumble' p 20

York, Jessica: 'Egyptian Spinach and Lentil Soup' p 17

Printed in the United Kingdom
by Lightning Source UK Ltd.
118823UK00001B/385-402